DEPARTMENT OF THE NAVY
HEADQUARTERS UNITED STATES MARINE CORPS
WASHINGTON, DC 20380-0001

I0500454

CAREER PLANNER TRAINING AND READINESS MANUAL

DEPARTMENT OF THE NAVY
HEADQUARTERS UNITED STATES MARINE CORPS
WASHINGTON, DC 20380-0001

MCO 3500.40
C 472
23 Mar 01

MARINE CORPS ORDER 3500.40

From: Commandant of the Marine Corps
To: Distribution List

Subj: CAREER PLANNER TRAINING AND READINESS MANUAL
      (SHORT TITLE: CAREER PLANNERS T&R MANUAL)

Encl: (1) Locator Sheet

1. <u>Purpose</u>. To publish revised training standards, regulations, and policies, which prescribe a career continuum of training, required of Career Planners.

2. <u>Background</u>. This Manual reflects a holistic approach to training Marine Corps Career Planners with a standardized career-training plan. The individual training standards contained in this Manual supersede the individual training standards listed in MCO 1510.100. That directive will remain in effect for approximately one year to support transition to the Career Planners T&R Manual by the Operating Forces and formal schools. This Manual incorporates both individual training standards and unit/section skills in a progressively more challenging "building block" approach that leaders can use to develop both the individual abilities and the team skills required of Career Planners.

3. <u>Reserve Applicability</u>. This Manual is applicable to the Marine Corps Reserve.

4. <u>Certification</u>. Reviewed and approved this date.

W. E. GASKIN
By direction

DISTRIBUTION: PCN 10203356600

    Copy to: 7000110 (55)
                7230080 (20)
                7000144/7230004/8145001

DISTRIBUTION STATEMENT A: Approved for public release; distribution is unlimited.

LOCATOR SHEET

Subj: _____

Location: _____
         (Indicate location(s) of copy(ies) of this annual.)

ENCLOSURE (1)

CAREER PLANNER T&R MANUAL

RECORD OF CHANGES

Log completed change action as indicated

Change Number	Date of Change	Date Entered	Signature of Person Incorporating Change

Chapter 1

Career Planner

CAREER PLANNERS T&R MANUAL

CHAPTER 1

Career Planner

                                                              PAGE

1001. INTRODUCTION.. 1-3

1002. UNIT TRAINING... 1-3

1003. THE HOLISTIC APPROACH TO TRAINING......................... 1-3

1004. THE CORE CAPABILITIES METHODOLOGY......................... 1-3

1005. CAREER PROGRESSION.. 1-3

1006. CAREER PROGRESSION PHILOSOPHY............................. 1-4

1007. EVALUATION OF TRAINING.................................... 1-4

1008. COMPONENTS OF A T&R EVENT................................. 1-4

1009. CRP COMPUTATION... 1-5

1010. INDIVIDUAL TASK MATRIX.................................... 1-6

1011. SECTION TASK MATRIX....................................... 1-6

1012. COMBAT CAPABLE TRAINING (100 LEVEL)....................... 1-6

1013. COMBAT READY TRAINING (200 LEVEL)......................... 1-6

1014. COMBAT QUALIFICATION TRAINING (300 LEVEL)................. 1-6

1015. SECTION SKILLS TRAINING (400 LEVEL)....................... 1-7

1016. SPECIAL DESIGNATIONS...................................... 1-7

1017. ACADEMIC TRAINING... 1-7

1018. CAREER PROFESSIONAL READING............................... 1-7

1019. UPDATE CHAINING... 1-7

1020. BILLETS REQUIRING FORMAL SCHOOL ATTENDANCE................ 1-7

1021. EXPENDABLE ORDNANCE REQUIREMENTS.......................... 1-7

1022. TRAINING REFERENCES....................................... 1-7

CHAPTER 1

APPENDIX

A   CORK CAPABILITIES

B   CAREER PROGRESSION PHILOSOPHY

C   BILLET APPLICABILITY

D   SECTION APPLICABILITY

E   COMBAT CAPABLE TRAINING (100 LEVEL)

F   COMBAT READY TRAINING (200 LEVEL)

G   COMBAT QUALIFICATION TRAINING (300 LEVEL)

H   SECTION TRAINING (400 LEVEL)

I   SPECIAL DESIGNATIONS

J   ACADEMIC TRAINING

K   CAREER PROFESSIONAL READING

L   EVENT CHAINING

M   BILLET REQUIRED FORMAL SCHOOLS

N   AMMUNITION REQUIREMENTS

O   REFERENCE LIST

CAREER PLANNERS T&R MANUAL

CHAPTER 1

Career Planner

1001. <u>INTRODUCTION</u>. The Training and Readiness (T&R) Manual is a comprehensive training document designed to identify training requirements and support resources for this Military Occupational Specialty (MOS). It replaces the Individual Training Standards (ITS)order as a training guide and provides trainers an immediate assessment of both individual and section combat readiness by assigning a Combat Readiness Percentage (CRP) to each training task. The T&R Manual also identifies tasks by billet applicability, enabling trainers to focus training in the appropriate areas.

1002. <u>UNIT TRAINING</u>

1. The heart of the T&R program lies in training Marines to perform as an integral unit in combat. Because unit readiness and individual readiness are directly related, the T&R Manual contains both individual training tasks and section training tasks. Individual training and the mastery of individual skills serve as the building blocks for unit combat readiness.

2. Guidance concerning unit training management and the process for establishing effective unit training management programs are contained in MCRP 3-OA, <u>Unit Training Management Guide (UTM)</u>.

1003. <u>THE HOLISTIC APPROACH TO TRAINING</u>. The T&R Manual combines traditional training such as military formal schools, Marine Corps Institute correspondence courses and Managed On-the-Job Training(MOJT), with nontraditional sources such as civilian college courses, other service correspondence courses, career professional reading, distance learning, and base training programs. This combination allows the flexibility to create a diverse training program capable of producing the best-trained Marine possible.

1004. <u>THE CORE CAPABILITIES METHODOLOGY</u>

1. **Core Tasks** are those essential basic skills that "make" a Marine and qualify that Marine for an MOS and are introduced in entry level training (100 level). **Core-Plus Tasks** are those advanced skills that are mission, rank, or billet specific, and are performed in the 200-300levels of training.

2. The tasks contained within this T&R Manual support a common set of skills derived from input by Subject Matter Experts (SME) and Operational Forces. These common skills provide a Core Capability shared by all Marines with like MOS, regardless of unit type or size.3. Core capabilities are contained in Appendix (A).

1005. <u>CAREER PROGRESSION</u>

CHAPTER 1

1.   100 level training (Combat Capable) is the initial MOS skills training at the formal school. At its completion, unit personnel are assigned basic MOS qualification and progress to the Combat Ready tier.

2.   200 level training (Combat Ready) trains newly schooled Marines and makes them _proficient_ in core capabilities. At its completion, unit personnel progress to the Combat Qualification tier.

3.   300 level training (Combat Qualification) produces combat leaders and fully qualified section members. The personnel who are being trained in the Combat Qualification tier are those Marines a commanding officer feels are capable of directing the actions of subordinates during wartime scenarios.

4.   400 level training (Section Skills) reflects section tasks that directly support the core capability list. They are group rather than individual in nature, and require participation by a section. 400 level tasks, when completed, provide training credit for those individual (200-300 levels) tasks utilized in the completion of the 400level task.

1006. CAREER PROGRESSION PHILOSOPHY. The career progression philosophy contained in Appendix (B) describes the typical training progression for a Marine of this MOS.

1007. EVALUATION OF TRAINING. Evaluation of the academic portions of the T&R Manual will be conducted either by written or oral examination or a combination of the two. A requirement to produce a product may accompany the task. Operational and system related tasks will be evaluated by practical application means, whenever possible. At the commander's discretion, a Marine may receive credit for task completion through an oral explanation of the steps or procedures involved rather than by physically performing the task.

1008. COMPONENTS OF A T&R EVENT

1.   General. An event contained within a T&R Manual is an individual or collective training standard and contains nine components.

> **EVENT CODE:** The code assigned to each task for ease of reference which identifies individual (100-300 level) or section tasks (400 level)

> **TASK:** A unit of work expressed as a performance-oriented action (i.e., "type a letter.").

> **CONDITION:** The constraints that affect the performance of the task in a real-world environment. It includes equipment, tools, materials, and

reference requirements and environmental and safety constraints pertaining to task completion.

STANDARD: The basis for judging the effectiveness of the task performance. It identifies the proficiency level for task performance in terms of accuracy, speed, sequencing, and adherence to procedural guidelines. It is not guidance; it is inviolate. Whenever possible, the standard should cite a reference that defines the task in procedural or operational terms.

CONCEPT OF TASK: This paragraph is optional but may be used if the task requires further explanation.

PREREQUISITE(S): A listing of academic training and/or other T&R events which must be completed prior to attempting completion of the task.

REFERENCE(S): A listing of doctrinal or reference publications which may assist the trainee in satisfying the performance standards and the trainer in evaluating the effectiveness of task completion.

ORDNANCE: A listing of ordnance types and quantities required to complete the task.

EXTERNAL SUPPORT REQUIREMENT(S): A listing of the external range, support aircraft, targets, training devices, or other personnel and equipment requirements needed for completion of the task.

1009. <u>CRP COMPUTATION</u>

1. Each task in the T&R Manual has an assigned Combat Readiness Percentage (CRP). The combined CRP total of the Individual tasks of the 100-300 level training is 100%. The breakdown of that 100% CRP for the Individual tasks is as follows: 100 level tasks taught at the Formal School have a total CRP value of 60%; 200 and 300 level tasks have a combined CRP value of 40%.

2. CRP for 400 level Section tasks is considered separately from the Individual 100-300 level task CRP values. 400 level section tasks have a total CR? value of 100% and are not considered in conjunction with the 100-300 level Individual task CRP values. A section that successfully performs its mission can achieve a satisfactory section CRP value even when it is severely undermanned or when the individual members of the section have low Individual CRP ratings in their 100-300 level training.

CHAPTER 1

1010. INDIVIDUAL TASK MATRIX

1.   The Individual Task Matrix, located at Appendix (C), summarizes the tasks that are applicable to specific billets. Utilizing the automated Training and Readiness Information Management System (ATRIMS) program and a syllabus tied to the event codes of the T&R Manual, trainers will quickly establish training priorities.

2.   Trainers can determine the training combat readiness of individual Marines by comparing the Marine's CRP combined total on the billet Specific completed 100-300 level tasks with the total possible CRP value of the Marine's billet. For example, if a billet has a total possible CRP value of 79.75% and an individual Marine's total CRP on completed 100-300 level tasks is 50%, a trainer can quickly determine which tasks must be addressed in order to raise the Marine's individual CRP to a higher level.

Components of the Individual Task Matrix Event Code - The code assigned to each task for ease of reference which identifies individual (100-300 level) tasks.

CRP (Combat Readiness Percentage) - Quantitative value assigned to each T&R task. Used to calculate Individual Combat Readiness Percentage.

Sustainment Interval (in months) - Denotes how frequently a Marine must demonstrate proficiency in the task.

Billet Applicability Checkmark - Specifies which T&R tasks pertain to each specific billet. Trainers can quickly focus each Marine's instruction on the specific tasks that match the Marine's Billet assignment.

Note 100 level Formal School training (Combat Capable Training)is applicable to all Marines who attend MOS producing schools.

1011.   SECTION TASK MATRIX. The Section Task Matrix, located at Appendix (D), summarizes the section tasks that are applicable to specific billets. It contains the same components as the Individual Task Matrix.

1012.   COMBAT CAPABLE TRAINING (100 level). 100 level tasks are contained in Appendix (E).

1013.   COMBAT READY TRAINING (200 level). 200 level tasks are contained in Appendix (F).

1014.   COMBAT QUALIFICATION TRAINING (300 level). 300 level tasks are contained in Appendix (G).

1015. SECTION SKILLS TRAINING (400 level). 400 level tasks are contained in Appendix (H)

1016. SPECIAL DESIGNATIONS. Completion of the courses of instruction contained in Appendix (I) qualifies the individual Marine for assignment to specialized billets and/or responsibilities.

1017. ACADEMIC TRAINING. The Academic Training contained in Appendix (J) lists civilian college courses, MCI courses, other service correspondence courses, etc., which are beneficial to professional development during 200-300 level training. They provide a Marine the opportunity to continue with professional development regardless of deployment status or workload.

1018. CAREER PROFESSIONAL READING. The Career professional Reading contained in Appendix (K) lists books that are recommended for professional development during 200-300 level training. These texts may be optional reading or may be tied to specific T&R tasks and require some type of product to be produced by the Marine.

1019. UPDATE CHAINING. Update chaining is contained in Appendix (L).

1020. BILLETS REQUIRING FORMAL SCHOOL ATTENDANCE. Billets, which require formal school attendance, are contained in Appendix (M).

1021. EXPENDABLE ORDNANCE REQUIREMENTS. Ordnance requirements are contained in Appendix (N), if required.

1022. TRAINING REFERENCES. The training references contained in Appendix (0) shall be utilized to determine task performance steps, grading criteria, and ensure standardization of training procedures.

Core Capabilities List

1. Identify, screen, and process Marines for reenlistment/extension/lateral move.

2. Identify, screen, and process Marines for special duty assignments.

3. Maintain the components of Systematic Career Planning.

4. Retain quality Marines to meet Marine Corps career force requirements.

5. Collects, collates, analyzes, and displays all statistical and historical retention data.

6. Serves as a subject matter expert for retention.

7. Responsible for Career Planning training progression.

8. Possess the professional communication skills to deliver persuasive/compelling public presentations.

9. Analyzes the unit's Systematic Career Planning techniques and develops plans to correct weaknesses and enhance strengths.

10. Educate Marines on Marine Corps opportunities and benefits.

11. Disseminate all information pertaining to retention in an automated and non-automated environment.

12. Screen applicants for lateral move into the Career Planning field.

13. Advise the commander on matters pertaining to retention.

14. Conduct counsultative needs-based interviews to identify a Marine's needs.

15. Match Marine Corps benefits to an individual Marines needs.

16. Coach commanders and senior enlisted unit members in the performance of their career planning responsibilities.

CHAPTER 1

APPENDIX B

CAREER PROGRESSION PHILOSOPHY

The Career Planning Force progression philosophy is based upon the application of Systematic Career Planning. A Marine selected for the Career Planning Force will attend the Basic Career Planners Course (BCPC),MCRD San Diego, CA. BCPC is 100 level training designed to provide basic instruction in the basic components of Systematic Career Planning; product knowledge, performance skills, and the contact to contract process. Upon graduation from BCPC the Marine will move into the 200 level of training. The 200 level of training is centered around formal schools and Managed On-the-Job Training (MOJT) and requires the Career Planner to apply the elements of Systematic Career Planning. The transition from 200 level training to 300 level training is marked by the attendance of the Advanced Career Planner Course (ACPC). ACPC is conducted at MCRD San Diego, CA and provides instruction in the advanced components of Systematic Career Planning; mentoring and development. Upon graduation of ACPC, the Marine will enter the 300 level of training. The 300 level of training is centered around formal schools and MOJT. During the 300 level of training the Marine will mentor, develop, and supervise Career Planners' in their application of Systematic Career Planning.

BILLET APPLICABILITY

Billets

A Batallion/Squadron Career Planner	N Processing Chief
B Group Career Planner	O Lat Move Chief
C Division Career Planner	P Base Career Planner
D MEF Career Planner	Q WING Career Planner
E	R MCAS Career Planner
F LANT Career Planner	S Regiment Career Planner
G TECOM Career Planner	T FSSG Career Planner
H MATCOM Career Planner	U Reserve Battalion/Squadron Career Planner
I	V Reserve Group/Regiment Career Planner
J MARFORRES Career Planner	W Reserve Small Unit Career Planner
K MCCDC Career Planner	X MCB Okinawa Career Planner
L Small Unit Career Planner	Y COMCAB East/West Career Planner
M Career Planner Liasion	Z

Event code	CRP	S/I (mo)	A	B	C	D	E	F	G	H	I	J	K	L	M	N	O	P	Q	R	S	T	U	V	W	X	Y	Z
200-CPC	0.81	.5	X	X	X	X	X	X	X	X	X	X	X	X	X	X	X	X	X	X	X	X	X	X	X	X	X	X
201-CPC	0.81	1	X	X									X					X		X	X	X	X		X	X	X	X	X
202-CPC	0.81	12	X	X									X					X		X	X	X	X		X	X	X	X	X
203-CPC	0.81	3	X	X									X					X		X	X	X	X		X	X	X		
204-CPR	0.81	3																			X	X	X		X	X	X		
205-CPC	0.27	1	X	X									X					X		X	X	X	X		X	X	X	X	X

CHAPTER 1

Event code	CRP	S/I (mo)	A	B	C	D	E	F	G	H	I	J	K	L	M	N	O	P	Q	R	S	T	U	V	W	X	Y	Z
206-CPC	0.27	6	X	X			X							X						X	X	X	X	X	X	X	X	
207-CPC	0.54	.5	X	X	X		X	X						X			X	X	X	X	X	X	X	X	X	X	X	X
208-CPC	0.27	1	X	X	X		X							X						X	X	X	X	X	X	X	X	X
209-CPC	0.54	1	X	X	X		X							X			X	X	X	X	X	X	X	X	X	X	X	X
210-CPR	0.54	12																						X	X			
211-CPC	0.27	12	X	X			X							X						X	X	X	X	X	X	X	X	X
212-CPC	0.54	3	X	X			X							X						X	X	X	X	X	X	X	X	X
213-CPC	0.27	.5	X	X	X	X	X	X	X				X	X			X			X	X	X	X	X	X	X	X	X
214-CPC	0.27	3	X	X			X							X						X	X	X	X	X	X	X	X	X
215-CPC	0.81	1	X	X			X							X						X	X	X	X	X	X	X	X	X
216-CPC	0.81	1	X	X			X							X						X	X	X	X	X	X	X	X	X
217-CPC	0.54	1	X	X			X							X						X	X	X	X	X	X	X	X	X
218-CPC	0.54	1	X	X			X							X						X	X	X	X	X	X	X	X	X
219-CPC	0.54	12	X	X			X	X						X						X	X	X	X	X	X	X	X	X
220-CPR	0.81	1																						X	X	X		
221-CPC	0.27	3	X	X	X		X	X						X						X	X	X	X	X	X	X	X	X
222-CPC	0.81	3	X	X	X		X							X						X	X	X	X	X	X	X	X	X
223-CPC	0.27	12	X	X	X	X	X	X				X	X	X	X	X	X	X	X	X	X	X	X	X	X	X	X	X
224-CPC	0.54	3	X	X	X		X	X				X	X	X	X	X	X	X	X	X	X	X	X	X	X	X	X	X
225-CPC	0.27	12	X	X	X		X	X				X	X	X	X	X	X	X	X	X	X	X	X	X	X	X	X	X
226-CPC	0.81	1	X	X			X							X						X	X	X	X	X	X	X	X	X

Event code	CRP	(mo) S/I	A	B	C	D	E	F	G	H	I	J	K	L	M	N	O	P	Q	R	S	T	U	V	W	X	Y	Z
227-CPC	0.54	3	X	X				X						X					X	X	X	X	X	X	X	X	X	X
228-CPC	0.54	3	X	X	X	X		X	X	X		X	X	X		X	X	X	X	X	X	X	X	X	X	X	X	X
229-CPC	0.27	12	X	X	X					X		X	X			X	X	X				X	X	X	X	X		
230-CPC	0.27	3	X	X				X					X							X	X	X	X	X	X	X		
231-CPR	0.54	6																			X	X	X	X	X			
232-CPR	0.27	12																			X	X	X	X	X			
233-CPR	0.54	12									X										X	X	X	X	X			
234-CPR	0.54	3																			X	X	X	X	X			
235-CPC	0.54	3	X	X				X						X	X				X	X	X	X	X	X	X	X	X	X
236-CPC	0.81	1	X	X	X	X		X	X	X		X	X	X	X	X	X	X	X	X	X	X	X	X	X	X	X	X
237-CPC	0.54	3	X	X	X	X		X	X	X		X	X	X	X	X	X	X	X	X	X	X	X	X	X	X	X	X
238-CPC	0.81	1	X	X				X						X	X	X	X	X	X	X	X	X	X	X	X	X		
239-CPC	0.81	.5	X	X				X						X	X	X	X	X	X	X	X	X	X	X	X	X		
240-CPC	0.81	1	X	X	X	X		X	X	X		X	X	X	X	X	X	X	X	X	X	X	X	X	X	X	X	X
241-CPC	0.54	1	X	X				X							X	X	X	X	X	X	X	X	X	X	X	X	X	X
242-CPC	0.81	1	X	X	X	X		X	X	X		X	X	X	X	X	X	X	X	X	X	X	X	X	X	X	X	X
243-CPC	0.27	6	X	X	X	X		X	X	X		X	X	X	X	X	X	X	X	X	X	X	X	X	X	X	X	X
244-CPC	0.54	12	X	X	X	X		X	X	X				X	X	X	X	X	X	X	X	X	X	X	X	X	X	X
245-CPC	0.27	3	X	X	X	X		X	X	X		X	X	X	X	X	X	X	X	X	X	X	X	X	X	X	X	X
246-CPC	0.27	1	X	X	X	X		X	X	X		X	X	X	X	X	X	X	X	X	X	X	X	X	X	X	X	X
247-CPC	0.27	1	X	X	X	X		X	X	X		X	X	X	X	X	X	X	X	X	X	X	X	X	X	X	X	X

CAREER PLANNERS T&R MANUAL

CHAPTER 1

Event code	CRP	S/I (mo)	A	B	C	D	E	F	G	H	I	J	K	L	M	N	O	P	Q	R	S	T	U	V	W	X	Y	Z
248-CPC	0.81	1	X	X	X		X	X	X	X		X	X	X				X	X	X	X	X	X	X	X	X	X	X	X
249-CPR	0.81	3																				X	X	X					
250-CPC	0.27	3	X	X	X		X	X	X			X	X	X	X	X	X	X			X	X	X	X	X	X	X		X
251-CPC	0.27	6	X	X				X						X		X	X	X		X	X	X	X	X	X	X	X	X	
252-CPC	0.81	.5	X	X	X		X	X	X	X	X	X	X	X	X	X	X	X	X	X	X	X	X	X	X	X	X	X	X
253-CPC	0.81	.5	X	X	X		X	X	X	X		X	X	X	X	X	X	X	X	X	X	X	X	X	X	X	X	X	X
300-CPA	0.54																												
301-CPA	0.81																												
302-CPA	0.27																												
303-CPA	0.54																												
304-CPA	0.27																												
305-CPA	0.27																												
306-CPA	0.27																												
307-CPA	0.81																												
308-CPA	0.81																												
309-CPA	0.54																												
310-CPA	0.81																												
311-CPA	0.27																												
312-CPA	0.54																												
313-CPA	0.27																												
314-CPA	0.27																												

Event code	CRP	S/I (mo)	A	B	C	D	E	F	G	H	I	J	K	L	M	N	O	P	Q	R	S	T	U	V	W	X	Y	Z
315-CPA	0.27																											
316-CPA	0.81																											
317-CPA	0.81																											
318-CPA	0.54																											
319-CPA	0.81																											
320-CPA	0.27																											
321-CPA	0.54																											
322-CPA	0.27																											
323-CPA	0.27																											
324-CPA	0.27																											
325-CPP	0.81	1	X	X	X			X	X	X		X										X	X	X	X	X	X	X	X
326-CPP	0.81	1	X	X	X			X	X	X		X	X	X	X	X	X	X	X	X	X	X	X	X	X	X	X	X	X
327-CPR	0.27	12																					X	X	X				
328-CPP	0.27	3	X	X	X			X	X	X		X		X	X	X	X	X	X	X	X	X	X	X	X	X	X	X	X
329-CPP	0.27	.5	X	X	X			X	X	X		X	X	X	X	X	X	X	X	X	X	X	X	X	X	X	X	X	X
330-CPP	0.54	3	X	X	X			X	X	X		X	X	X	X	X	X	X	X	X	X	X	X	X	X	X	X	X	X
331-CPR	0.27	12										X													X	X	X		
332-CPP	0.81	1	X	X	X			X	X	X		X	X	X	X	X	X	X	X	X	X	X	X	X	X	X	X	X	X
333-CPP	0.81	.5	X	X	X			X	X	X		X	X	X	X	X	X	X	X	X	X	X	X	X	X	X	X	X	X
334-CPP	0.81	12	X	X	X			X	X	X		X	X	X							X	X	X	X	X	X	X	X	X
335-CPP	0.27	6	X	X	X			X	X	X		X	X	X							X	X	X	X	X	X	X	X	X

CAREER PLANNERS T&R MANUAL

CHAPTER 1

Event code	CRP	S/I (mo)	A	B	C	D	E	F	G	H	I	J	K	L	M	N	O	P	Q	R	S	T	U	V	W	X	Y	Z
336-CPP	0.81	12	X	X	X	X	X	X	X	X	X	X	X				X	X	X	X	X	X	X	X	X	X	X	X
337-CPR	0.54	6							X														X	X	X			
338-CPP	0.81	3	X	X	X		X	X	X	X	X	X					X	X	X	X	X	X					X	X
339-CPA	0.81	3																										
340-CPP	0.81	1								X				X	X	X												
341-CPP	0.54	1														X												
342-CPP	0.27	3														X												
343-CPP	0.27	3														X												
344-CPP	0.54	.5												X	X	X												
345-CPP	0.81	1												X	X	X												
346-CPR	0.27	3								X																		
347-CPR	0.54	12								X																		

CAREER PLANNERS T&R MANUAL

CHAPTER 1

APPENDIX D

SECTION APPLICABILITY

Sections

1 Reenlistment Unit
2
3
4
5
6
7
8
9
10
11
12
13

14
15
16
17
18
19
20
21
22
23
24
25
26

Event code	CRP	(mo) S/I	1	2	3	4	5	6	7	8	9	10	11	12	13	14	15	16	17	18	19	20	21	22	23	24	25	26
400-CPP	0.25	3	X																									
401-CPP	0.25	3	X																									
402-CPP	0.25	3	X																									
404-CPP	0.25	3	X																									

CHAPTER 1

APPENDIX E

COMBAT CAPABLE TRAINING (100 LEVEL)

Purpose: The Career Planning Force progression philosophy is based upon the application of Systematic Career Planning. A Marine selected for the Career Planning Force will attend the Basic Career Planners Course (BCPC), MCRD San Diego, CA. BCPC is 100 level training designed to provide basic instruction in the basic components of Systematic Career Planning; product knowledge, performance skills, and the contact to contract process. Upon graduation from BCPC the Marine will move into the 200 level of training.

Administrative Notes: None.

Prerequisites: None.

Event code: 100-CPC

Task: Verify Marine's qualifications for reenlistment.

Condition: provided with the appropriate references, materials, and equipment

Standard: Per the appropriate references.

Concept of task: None.

Prerequisites: None.

CRP: 0 **Sustainment Interval (months):** 0

External Support Required: None.

Events updated: None.

Reference(s): MCO P1040.31, Enlisted Career planning and Retention Manual
MCO P1040R.35, Reserve Career Planning and Retention Manual

Event code: 101-CPC

Task: Determine a Marine's moral qualifications for reenlistment.

Condition: Provided with the appropriate references, materials, and equipment.

Standard: Per the appropriate references.

Concept of task: None.

Prerequisites: None.

CRP: 0 **Sustainment Interval (months):** 0

External Support Required: None.

Events updated: None.

Reference(s): MCO P1040.31, Enlisted Career Planning and Retention Manual
MCO P1040R.35, Reserve Career Planning and Retention Manual

Event code: 102-CPC

Task: Determine a Marine's physical qualifications for reenlistment.

Condition: Provided with the appropriate references, materials, and equipment.

Standard: Per the appropriate references.

Concept of task: None.

Prerequisites: None.

CRP: 0 **Sustainment Interval (months):** 0

CHAPTER 1

External Support Required: None.

Events updated: None.

Reference(s): MCO P1040R.35, Reserve Career Planning and Retention Manual
MCO 6100.10, weight Control and Military Appearance
MCO 6100.3, Physical Fitness
MCO P1040.31, Enlisted Career Planning and Retention Manual

Event code: 103-CPC

Task: Determine a Marine's education qualifications.

Condition: Provided with the appropriate references, materials, and equipment.

Standard: Per the appropriate references.

Concept of task: None.

Prerequisites: None.

CRP: 0 **Sustainment Interval (months)**: 0

External Support Required: None.

Events updated: None.

Reference(s): MCO P1040R.35, Reserve Career Planning and Retention Manual
MCO P1040.31, Enlisted Career Planning and Retention Manual

Event code: 104-CPC

Task: Determine a Marine's mental qualifications.

Condition: Provided with the appropriate references, materials, and equipment.

Standard: Per the appropriate references.

Concept of task: None.

Prerequisites: None.

CRP: 0 **Sustainment Interval (months)**: 0

External Support Required: None.

Events updated: None.

Reference(s): MCO P1040R.35, Reserve Career Planning and Retention Manual
MCO P1040.31, Enlisted Career Planning and Retention Manual

CHAPTER 1

Event code: 105-CPC

Task: Determine a Marine's dependent status.

Condition: Provided with the appropriate references, materials, and Equipment.

Standard: MCO P1080.20, Marine Corps Total Forces Codes Manual.

Concept of task: None.

Prerequisites: None

CRP: 0 **Sustainment Interval (months):** 0

External Support Required: None.

Events updated: None.

Reference(s): MCO P1040.31, Enlisted Career Planning and Retention Manual

Event code: 106-CPC

Task: Determine a Marine's statement of service.

Condition: Provided with the appropriate references, materials, and equipment.

Standard: Per the appropriate references.

Concept of task: None.

Prerequisites: None.

CRP: 0 **Sustainment Interval (months):** 0

External Support Required: None.

Events updated: None.

Reference(s): MCO P1080.40 Personnel Reporting Instructions Manual (PRIM)
MCO P1900.16, Marine Corps Separation and Retirement Manual (SEPMAN}
MCO P7220.31, Joint Uniform Military Pay System Field Procedures Manual
Department of Defense Pay Entitlements Manual (DODPM)

Event code: 107-CPC

Task: List the procedures for processing a Marine's Reenlistment/Extension Lateral Move (RELM) request.

Condition: Provided with the appropriate references, materials, and equipment.

Standard: Per the appropriate references.

Concept of task: None.

Prerequisites: None.

E-4

CRP: 0   **Sustainment Interval (months):** 0

External Support Required: None.

Events updated: None.

Reference(s): MCO P1040R.35, Reserve Career Planning and Retention Manual
MCO P1040.31, Enlisted Career Planning and Retention Manual

Event code: 108-CPC

Task: Prepare a RELM.

Condition: Provided with the appropriate references, materials, and equipment.

Standard: Per the appropriate references.

Concept of task: None.

Prerequisites: None.

CRP: 0   **Sustainment Interval (months):** 0

External Support Required: None.

Events updated: None.

Reference(s): MCO P1040R.35, Reserve Career Planning and Retention Manual
MCO P1040.31, Enlisted Career Planning and Retention Manual

Event code: 110-CPC

Task: Explain Marine Corps benefits.

Condition: Provided with the appropriate references, materials, and utilizing the Marine Corps Opportunities Book (Career Planner Edition)(MCOB-CP).

Standard: Per the appropriate references.

Concept of task: None.

Prerequisites: None.

CRP: 0   **Sustainment Interval (months):** 0

External Support Required: None.

Events updated: None.

Reference(s): MCO 1560.15, Marine Corps Enlisted Commissioning Education Program (MCECP)
MCO 1560.21, Degree Completion Program for Staff Noncommissioned Officers
MCO P1040R.35, Reserve Career Planning and Retention Manual

CHAPTER 1

Event code: 111-CPR

Task: Explain the Mandatory Drill Stop Date (MDSD).

Condition: Provided with the appropriate references, materials, and equipment.

Standard: MCO P1040R.35, Reserve Career Planning and Retention Manual.

Concept of task: None.

Prerequisites: None.

CRP: 0   **Sustainment Interval (months):**   0

External Support Required: None.

Events updated: None.

Reference(s): MCO P1040.31, Enlisted Career Planning and Retention Manual

Event code: 112-CPC

Task: Explain the organizational structure of the career planning force.

Condition: Provided with the appropriate references, materials, and equipment.

Standard: Per the appropriate references.

Concept of task: None.

Prerequisites: None.

CRP: 0   **Sustainment Interval (months):**   0

External Support Required: None.

Event updated: None.

Reference(s): MCO P1040.31, Enlisted Career Planning and Retention Manual
MCO P1040R.35, Reserve Career Planning and Retention Manual

Event code: 113-CPC

Task: Explain Enlisted Career Force Control (ECFC) policies.

Condition: Provided with the appropriate references, materials, and equipment.

Standard: Per the appropriate references.

Concept of task: None.

Prerequisites: None.
CRP: 0   **Sustainment Interval (months):**   0

External Support Required: None.

CHAPTER 1

Events updated: None.

Reference(s): MC Bul 5314, Series Enlisted Career Force Controls (ECFC)
MCO P1040R.35, Reserve Career Planning and Retention Manual
MCO P1040.31, Enlisted Career Planning and Retention Manual

Event code: 114-CPC

Task: Explain the basic correspondence procedures for career planning.

Condition: provided with the appropriate references, materials, and equipment.

Standard: SECNAVINST 5216.5, Correspondence Manual.

Concept of task: None.

Prerequisites: None.

CRP: 0   **Sustainment Interval (months):** 0

External Support Required: None.

Events updated: None.

Reference(s): SECNAVINST 5216.5, Correspondence Manual

Event code: 115-CPC

Task: Explain the elements of the Service Record Book (SRB).

Condition: provided with the appropriate references, materials, and equipment.

Standard: Per the appropriate references.

Concept of task: None.

Prerequisites: None

CRP: 0   **Sustainment Interval (months):** 0

External Support Required: None.

Events updated: None.

Reference(s): MCO P1070.12, Marine Corps Individual Records Administration Manual (IRAM)
MCO P1001R.1, Marine Corps Reserve Administration Management Manual (MCRAMM)

Event code: 116-CPC

Task: Calculate pay and allowances as it pertains to Career Planning.

Condition: Provided with the appropriate references, materials, and equipment.

Standard: Per the appropriate references.

Concept of task: None.

Prerequisites: None.

CRP: 0   **Sustainment Interval (months):** 0

External Support Required: None.

Events updated: None.

Reference(s): Department of Defense Pay Entitlements Manual (DODPM)
Department of Defense Financial Management Regulation (DODFMR)
MCO 7220.31, Joint Uniform Military Pay System Field Procedures Manual

Event code: 117-CPC

Task: Explain the First Term Alignment Plan (FTAP)

Condition: Provided with the appropriate references, materials, and equipment.

Standard: Per the appropriate references.

Concept of task: None.

Prerequisites: None.

CRP: 0   **Sustainment Interval (months):** 0

External Support Required: None.

Events updated: None.

Reference(s): MCO P1040R.35, Reserve Career Planning and Retention Manual
MCO P1040.31, Enlisted Career Planning and Retention Manual

Event code: 118-CPC

Task: Navigate in the Total Force Retention System.

Condition: provided with the appropriate references, materials, and equipment.

Standard: Per the appropriate references.

Concept of task: None.

Prerequisites: None.

CRP: 0   **Sustainment Interval (months):** 0

External Support Required: None.

Events updated: None.

Reference(s): MCO P1040R.35, Reserve Career Planning and Retention Manual

CHAPTER 1

MCO P1040.31, Enlisted Career Planning and Retention Manual

Event code: 119-CPC

Task: Calculate Lump Sum Leave (LSL).

Condition: Provided with the appropriate references, materials, and equipment.

Standard: Per the appropriate references.

Concept of task: None.

Prerequisites: None.

CRP: 0 **Sustainment Interval (months):** 0

External Support Required: None.

Events updated: None.

Reference(s): Department of Defense Financial Management Regulation (DODFMR)
MCO P1050.3, Leave and Liberty Manual
MCO P7220.31, Joint Uniform Military Pay System Field Procedures Manual

Event code: 120-CPC
Task: Explain HUMS as it pertains to Career Planning.

Condition: Provided with the appropriate references, materials, and Equipment

Standard: MCO P1700.24, Marine Corps Family Services Standard Operating Procedure.

Concept of task: None.

Prerequisites: None.

CRP: 0 **Sustainment Interval (months):** 0

External Support Required: None.

Events updated: None.

Reference(s): MCO P1700.24, Marine Corps Family Services Standard Operating Procedure.

Event code: 121-CPC

Task: Explain the Exceptional Family Member Program (EFMP).

Condition: Provided with the appropriate references, materials, and equipment.

Standard: MCO P1700.24, Marine Corps Family Services Standard Operating Procedure.

Concept of task: None.

Prerequisites: None

CRP: 0   **Sustainment Interval (months)**: 0

External Support Required: None.

Events updated: None.

Reference(s): MCO P1700.24, Marine Corps Family Services Standard
                   Operating Procedure.

Event code: 122-CPC

Task: Navigate in the Marine Corps Total Force System (MCTFS).

Condition: Provided with the appropriate references, materials, and
                equipment.

Standard: Per the appropriate references.

Concept of task: None.

Prerequisites: None.

CRP: 0   **Sustainment Interval (months)**: 0

External Support Required: None.

Events updated: None.

Reference(s): MCO P1040R.35, Reserve Career Planning and Retention Manual
                   MCO P1040.31, Enlisted Career Planning and Retention
                   Manual

Event code: 123-CPC

Task: Explain the Lateral Move Program.

Condition: Provided with the appropriate references, materials, and
                equipment.

Standard: MCO 1220.5. Enlisted Lateral Movement.

Concept of task: None.

Prerequisites: None.

CRP: 0   **Sustainment Interval (months)**: 0

External Support Required: None.

Events updated: None.

Reference(s): MCO 1220.5, Enlisted Lateral Movement

Event code: 124-CPC

Task: Explain the Overseas Extension Programs (OEP).

Condition: Provided with the appropriate references, materials, and equipment.

Standard: Per the appropriate references.

Concept of task: None.

Prerequisites: None.

CRP: 0 **Sustainment Interval (months):** 0

External Support Required: None.

Events updated: None.

Reference(s): MCO 1220.5, Enlisted Lateral Movement
MCO P1040.31, Enlisted Career Planning and Retention Manual

Event code: 125-CPC

Task: Explain the Performance Evaluation System as it pertains to Career Planning.

Condition: Provided with the appropriate references, materials, and equipment.

Standard: Per the appropriate references.

Concept of task: None.

Prerequisites: None.

CRP: 0 **Sustainment Interval (months):** 0

External Support Required: None.

Events updated: None.

Reference(s): MCO 1610.11, Performance Evaluation Appeals
MCO P1610.7, Performance Evaluation System (PES)
MCO P1040.31, Enlisted Career Planning and Retention Manual

Event code: 126-CPC

Task: Explain the reserve opportunities available to transitioning Marines.

Condition: Provided with the appropriate references, materials, and utilizing the Marine Corps Opportunities Book (Career Planner Edition) (MCOB-CP).

Standard: Per the appropriate references.

Concept of task: None.

Prerequisites: None.

CRP: 0 **Sustainment Interval (months):** 0

External Support Required: None.

Events updated: None.

Reference(s):   MCO P1040R.35, Reserve Career planning and Retention
Manual
MCO P1040.31, Enlisted Career planning and Retention
Manual
MCO 1001.39, Counseling of Enlisted Personnel being
Separated from Active Duty in the Marine Corps Concerning
Participation in the Marine Corps Reserve

Event code: 127-CPC

Task: Explain the Marine Corps promotion policies as it pertains to
Career Planning.

Condition: Provided with the appropriate references, materials, and
equipment.

Standard: Per the appropriate references.

Concept of task: None.

Prerequisites: None.

CRP: 0   **Sustainment Interval (months):**   0

External Support Required: None.

Events updated: None.

Reference(s):   MCO P1400.32, Enlisted Promotion Manual

Event code: 128-CPC

Task: Apply interpersonal communications skills.

Condition: Provided with the appropriate references, materials, and
equipment.

Standard: Achieve Global.

Concept of task: None.

Prerequisites: None.

CRP: 0   **Sustainment Interval (months):**   0

External Support Required: None.

Events updated: None.

Reference(s):   Achieve Global products

Event code: 129-CPC

Task: Complete an agreement to extend enlistment form (NAVMC 321a).

Condition: Provided with the appropriate references, materials, and
equipment.

Standard: Per the appropriate references.

Concept of task: None.

Prerequisites: None.

CRP: 0   **Sustainment Interval (months):** 0

External Support Required: None.

Events updated: None.

Reference(s): MCO P1070.12, Marine Corps Individual Records
Administration Manual (IRAM)
MCO P1001R.1, Marine Corps Reserve Administration
Management Manual (MCRMMM)

Event code: 130-CPC

Task: Complete a reenlistment contract (DD form 4).

Condition: provided with the appropriate references, materials, and
equipment.

Standard: Per the appropriate references.

Concept of task: None.

Prerequisites: None.

CRP: 0   **Sustainment Interval (months):** 0

External Support Required: None.

Events updated: None.

Reference(s): MCO P1070.12, Marine Corps Individual Records
Administration Manual (IRAM)
MCO P1001R.1, Marine Corps Reserve Administration
Management Manual (MCRAMM)

Event code: 131-CPC

Task: Conduct a reenlistment ceremony.

Condition: Provided with the appropriate references, materials, and
equipment.

Standard: Per the appropriate references.

Concept of task: None.

Prerequisites: None.

CRP: 0   **Sustainment Interval (months):** 0

External Support Required: None.

Events updated: None.

Reference(s): MCO P1040R.35, Reserve Career Planning and Retention Manual
MCO P1040.31, Enlisted Career Planning and Retention
Manual   E-13

Event code: 132-CPC

Task: Complete required reenlistment certificates.

Condition: Provided with the appropriate references, materials, and equipment.

Standard: Per the appropriate references.

Concept of task: None.

Prerequisites: None.

CRP: 0 **Sustainment Interval (months):** 0

External Support Required: None.

Events updated: None.

Reference(s): MCO P1040R.35, Reserve Career Planning and Retention Manual
MCO P1040.31, Enlisted Career Planning and Retention Manual
MCO P1900.16, Marine Corps Separation and Retirement Manual (SEPMAN)

Event code: 133-CPC

Task: Explain involuntarily separations pay eligibility.

Condition: Provided with the appropriate references, materials, and utilizing the Marine Corps Opportunities Book (Career Planner Edition)(MCOB-CP).

Standard: Per the appropriate references.

Concept of task: None.

Prerequisites: None.

CRP: 0 **Sustainment Interval (months):** 0

External Support Required: None.

Events updated: None.

Reference(s): MCO P1040R.35, Reserve Career Planning and Retention Manual
MCO P1040.31, Enlisted Career Planning and Retention Manual
MCO P1900.16, Marine Corps Separation and Retirement Manual (SEPMAN)

Event code: 134-CPC

Task: Explain the mission of the Career Planning force.

Condition: provided with the appropriate references, materials, and equipment.

Standard: Per the appropriate references.

Concept of task: None.

Prerequisites: None.

CRP: 0 **Sustainment Interval (months):** 0

External Support Required: None.

Events updated: None.

Reference(s): MCO P1040R.35, Reserve Career Planning and Retention Manual
MCO P1040.31, Enlisted Career Planning and Retention Manual

Event code: 135-CPC

Task: Apply professional Selling Skills.

Condition: Provided with the appropriate references, materials, and equipment.

Standard: Achieve Global.

Concept of task: None.

Prerequisites: None.

CRP: 0 **Sustainment Interval (months):** 0

External Support Required: None.

Events updated: None.

Reference(s): Achieve Global products

Event code: 136-CPC

Task: Conduct required interviews.

Condition: Provided with the appropriate references, materials, and utilizing the Marine Corps Opportunities Book (Career planner Edition) (MCOB-CP).

Standard: Per the appropriate references.

Concept of task: None.

Prerequisites: None.

CRP: 0 **Sustainment Interval (months):** 0

External Support Required: None.

Events updated: None.

Reference(s): MCO P1040R.35, Reserve Career Planning and Retention Manual
MCO P1040.31, Enlisted Career Planning and Retention

Manual

Event code: 137-CPC

Task: Demonstrate communication skills.

Condition: provided with the appropriate references, materials, and equipment.

Standard: Achieve Global.

Concept of task: None.

Prerequisites: None.

CRP: 0 **Sustainment Interval (months):** 0

External Support Required: None.

Events updated: None.

Reference(s): Achieve Global products

Event code: 138-CPC

Task: Explain the Marine Corps personnel assignment policy.

Condition: Provided with the appropriate references, materials, and utilizing the Marine Corps Opportunities Book (Career Planner Edition) (MCOB-CP).

Standard: Per the appropriate references.

Concept of task: None.

Prerequisites: None.

CRP: 0 **Sustainment Interval (months):** 0

External Support Required: None.

Events updated: None.

Reference(s): MCO P1300.8, Marine Corps Personnel Assignment Policy
MCO P1000.6, Assignment, Classification, and Travel Systems Manual (ACTSMAN)

Event code: 139-CPC

Task: Explain educational opportunities.

Condition: Provided with the appropriate references, materials, and utilizing the Marine Corps Opportunities Book (Career Planner Edition) (MCOB-CP).

Standard: Per the appropriate references.

Concept of task: None.

Prerequisites: None.

CRP: 0   **Sustainment Interval (months):**   0

External Support Required: None.

Events updated: None.

Reference(s): MCO 1560.21, Staff Noncommissioned Officer Degree
              Completion Program (SNCODCP)
              MCO 1560.24, Broadened Opportunity for Officer Selection
              and Training Program (BOOST)
              MCO 1560R.30, Selected Reserve Montgomery GI Bill (MOIB-R)
              MCO 1560.26, Marine Corps Tuition Assistance Program
              MCO 1560.28, Veterans Educational Assistance Program (VEAP)
              MCO 1550.22, Marine Corps Apprenticeship Program

Event code: 140-CPC

Task: Explain the reenlistment incentives.

Condition: Provided with the appropriate references, materials, and
            utilizing the Marine Corps Opportunities Book (Career Planner
            Edition) (MCOB-CP).

Standard: Per the appropriate references.

Concept of task: None.

Prerequisites: None.

CRP: 0   **Sustainment Interval (months):**   0

External Support Required: None.

Events updated: None.

Reference(s): MCO 7220R.38, Selected Reserve Incentive Program (SRIP)
              MCO 7220.24, Selective Reenlistment Bonus Program (SRBP)
              MCO 1220.5, Enlisted Lateral Movement

Event code: 141-CPC

Task: Explain the Selective Reenlistment Bonus Program (SRBP).

Condition: Provided with the appropriate references, materials, and
            utilizing the Marine Corps Opportunities Book (Career Planner
            Edition) (MCOB-CP).

Standard: MCO 7220.24, Selective Reenlistment Bonus Program(SRBP).

Concept of task: None.

Prerequisites: None.

CRP: 0   **Sustainment Interval (months):**   0

External Support Required: None.

Events updated: None.

CHAPTER 1

Reference(s): MCO 7220.24, Selective Reenlistment Bonus Program (SRBP)

Event code: 142-CPC

Task: Explain the Reserve Optional Enlistment Program (ROEP)

Condition: Provided with the appropriate references, materials, and utilizing the Marine Corps Opportunities Book (Career Planner Edition) (MCOB-CP)

Standard: MCO 1133R.2E, Reserve Optional Enlistment Program (ROEP).

Concept of task: None.

Prerequisites: None.

CRP: 0   **Sustainment Interval (months):**   0

External Support Required: None.

Events updated: None.

Reference(s): MCO 1133R.26, Reserve Optional Enlistment Program (ROEP)

Event code: 143-CPC

Task: Navigate in the Message Dissemination System (MDS)

Condition: Provided with the appropriate references, materials,and equipment.

Standard: Message Dissemination System (MDS) users manual.

Concept of task: None.

Prerequisites: None.

CRP: 0   **Sustainment Interval (months):**   0

External Support Required: None.

Events updated: None.

Reference(s): Message Dissemination System (MDS) users manual

Event code: 144-CPC

Task: Explain the Apprenticeship Program.

Condition: Provided with the appropriate references, materials, and utilizing the Marine Corps Opportunities Book (Career Planner Edition)(MCOB-CP).

Standard: MCO 1550.22, Marine Corps Apprenticeship Program.

Concept of task: None.

Prerequisites: None.

CRP: 0   **Sustainment Interval (months):**   0

External Support Required: None.

Events updated: None.

Reference(s): MCO 1550.22, Marine Corps Apprenticeship Program

Event code: 145-CPC

Task: List the components of Systematic Career Planning.

Condition: Provided with the appropriate references, materials, and equipment

Standard: Per the appropriate references.

Concept of task: None.

Prerequisites: None.

CRP: 0   **Sustainment Interval (months):** 0

External Support Required: None.

Events updated: None.

Reference(s): MCO P1040R.35, Reserve Career Planning and Retention Manual
MCO P1040.31, Enlisted Career Planning and Retention Manual

Event code: 146-CPR

Task: List the steps necessary to maintain the Reserve Referral Credit Program.

Condition: Provided with the appropriate references, materials, and equipment.

Standard: MCO 1130.56, Total Force Recruiting.

Concept of task: None.

Prerequisites: None.

CRP: 0   **Sustainment Interval (months):** 0

External Support Required: None.

Events updated: None.

Reference(s): MCO 1130.56, Total Force Recruiting

Event code: 147-CPC

Task: List the steps necessary to maintain the Media Program.

Condition: Provided with the appropriate references, materials, and equipment.

Standard: MCO 1130.56, Total Force Recruiting.

Concept of task: None.

Prerequisites: None.

CRP: 0 **Sustainment Interval (months):** 0

External Support Required: None.

Events updated: None.

Reference(s): MCO 1130.56, Total Force Recruiting

Event code: 146-CPC

Task: Identify the elements of the working file.

Condition: Provided with the appropriate references, materials, and Equipment

Standard: Per the appropriate references.

Concept of task: None.

Prerequisites: None

CRP: 0 **Sustainment Interval (months):** 0

External Support Required: None.

Events updated: None.

Reference(s): MCO P104OR.35, Reserve Career Planning and Retention Manual
MCO P1040.31, Enlisted Career Planning and Retention Manual

Event code: 149-CPC

Task: Conduct a Telephone Call (TC)

Condition: Provided with the appropriate references, materials, and utilizing the Marine Corps Opportunities Book (Career Planner Edition) (MCOBCP).

Standard: Achieve Global.

Concept of task: Focus includes phone calls to senior HQ/Monitors.

Prerequisites: None.

CRP: 0 **Sustainment Interval (months):** 0

External Support Required: None.

Events updated: None.

Reference(s): Achieve Global products

Event code: 150-CPC

Task: Identify the requirements for conducting Area Canvassing (AC)

Condition: Provided with the appropriate references, materials, and utilizing the Marine Corps Opportunities Book (Career Planner Edition) (MCOB-CP).

Standard: Achieve Global.

Concept of task: None.

Prerequisites: None.

CRP: 0 **Sustainment Interval (months):** 0

External Support Required: None.

Events updated: None.

Reference(s): Achieve Global products

Event code: 151-CPC

Task: Identify the requirements for handling Office Traffic (OT).

Condition: provided with the appropriate references, materials, and utilizing the Marine Corps Opportunities Book (Career Planner Edition) (MCOB-CP).

Standard: Achieve Global.

Concept of task: None.

Prerequisites: None.

CRP: 0 **Sustainment Interval (months):** 0

External Support Required: None.

Events updated: None.

Reference(s): Achieve Global products

Event code: 153-CPC

Task: Identify the elements of time management.

Condition: Provided with the appropriate references, materials, and equipment.

Standard: Achieve Global.

Concept of task: None.

Prerequisites: None.

CRP: 0 **Sustainment Interval (months):** 0

External Support Required: None.

Events updated: None.

Reference(s): Achieve Global products

Event code: 154-CPC

Task: Analyze Career Planning data.

Condition: Provided with the appropriate references, materials, and equipment.

Standard: Per the appropriate references.

Concept of task: None.

Prerequisites: None.

CRP: 0   **Sustainment Interval (months):** 0

External Support Required: None.

Events updated: None.

Reference(s): MCO P1040R.35, Reserve Career Planning and Retention Manual
MCO P1040.31, Enlisted Career Planning and Retention Manual

Event code: 155-CPC

Task: List the elements associated with automated Career Planning.

Condition: provided with the appropriate references, materials, and equipment.

Standard: Per the appropriate references.

Concept of task: None.

Prerequisites: None.

CRP: 0   **Sustainment Interval (months):** 0

External Support Required: None.

Events updated: None.

Reference(s): MCO P1040R.35, Reserve Career Planning and Retention Manual
MCO P1040.31, Enlisted Career Planning and Retention Manual

Event code: 156-CPC

Task: Explain enlisted to officer programs.

Condition: provided with the appropriate references, materials, and utilizing the Marine Corps Opportunities Book (Career Planner Edition) (MCOB-CP).

Standard: Per the appropriate references.

Concept of task: None.

Prerequisites: None.

CRP: 0   **Sustainment Interval (months):** 0

External Support Required: None.

Events updated: None.

Reference(s): MCO 1530.11, Naval Academy/Naval Preparatory School
MCO 1560.15, Marine Corps Enlisted Commissioning

Education Program (MECEP)
MCO 1040.42, LDO/WO Program
MCO 1040.43, Enlisted to Officer Commissioning Programs
(ECP/MCP)
MCO 1040R.10, Selected Marine Corps Reserve Direct
Commissioning Program (SMCRDCP)

Event code: 157-CPC

Task: List the procedures for processing special duty
assignments.

Condition: Provided with the appropriate references, materials,
and utilizing the Marine Corps Opportunities Book (Career
Planner Edition) (MCOB-CP).

Standard: Per the appropriate references.

Concept of task: None.

Prerequisites: None.

CRP: 0   **Sustainment Interval (months):** 0

External Support Required: None.

Events updated: None.

Reference(s): MCO P1326.6, Selection Screening and Preparation of
Enlisted Marines for Assignment to Drill
MCO 7220.12, Special Duty Assignment Pay Program

Event code: 155-CPC

Task: Complete an Administrative Action (AA) Form.

Condition: Provided with the appropriate references, materials, and
equipment.

Standard: Per the appropriate references.

Concept of task: None.

Prerequisites: None.

CRP: 0   **Sustainment Interval (months):** 0

External Support Required: None.

Events updated: None.

Reference(s): SECNAVINST 5216.5, Correspondence Manual
MCO P1070.12, Marine Corps Individual Records
Administration Manual (IRAM)

Event code: 159-CPC

Task: Explain the initial interview.

Condition: Provided with the appropriate references, materials, and
equipment.

Standard: Per the appropriate references.

Concept of task: Explain to both the Active and Reserve aspects (TIME FRAME)

Prerequisites: None.

CRP: 0 **Sustainment Interval (months):** 0

External Support Required: None.

Events updated: None.

Reference(s): MCO P1040R.35, Reserve Career Planning and Retention Manual
MCO P1040.31, Enlisted Career Planning and Retention Manual

Event code: 180-CPC

Task: Complete a Naval Message.

Condition: Provided with the appropriate references, materials, and equipment.

Standard: SECNAVINST 5216.5, Correspondence Manual.

Concept of task: None.

Prerequisites: None.

CRP: 0 **Sustainment Interval (months):** 0

External Support Required: None.

Events updated: None.

Reference(s): SECNAVINST 5216.5, Correspondence Manual

Event code: 161-CPC

Task: List the elements of command relations.

Condition: Provided with the appropriate references, materials, and equipment.

Standard: Per the appropriate references.

Concept of task: None.

Prerequisites: None.

CRP: 0 **Sustainment Interval (months):** 0

External Support Required: None.

Events updated: None.

Reference(s): SECNAVINST 5216.5, Correspondence Manual

Event code: 162-CPC

Task: Explain the prerequisites for reenlistment.

Condition: Provided with the appropriate references, materials, and utilizing the Marine Corps Opportunities Book (Career Planner Edition) (MCOB-CP).

Standard: Per the appropriate references.

Concept of task: None.

Prerequisites: None

CRP: 0 **Sustainment Interval (months):** 0

External Support Required: None.

Events updated: None.

Reference(s): MCO P1040R.35, Reserve Career Planning and Retention Manual
MCO P1040.31, Enlisted Career Planning and Retention Manual

Event code: 163-CPC

Task: Employ collateral material during a sales presentation.

Condition: Provided with the appropriate references, materials, and utilizing the Marine Corps Opportunities Book (Career Planner Edition) (MCOB-CP).

Standard: Achieve Global.

Concept of task: None.

Prerequisites: None.

CRP: 0 **Sustainment Interval (months):** 0

External Support Required: None.

Events updated: None.

Reference(s): Achieve Global products

Event code: 164-CPC

Task: Explain the Quality Reenlistment Program (QRP).

Condition: Provided with the appropriate references, materials, and utilizing the Marine Corps Opportunities Book (Career Planner Edition) (MCOB-CP).

Standard: MCO P1040.31, Enlisted Career Planning and Retention Manual.

Concept of task: None.

Prerequisites: None.

CRP: 0 **Sustainment Interval (months):** 0

External Support Required: None.

Events updated: None.

Reference(s): MCO P1040.31, Enlisted Career Planning and Retention
Manual

Event code: 165-CPC

Task: List the requirements for maintaining the Career Planning Contact
Record.

Condition: Provided with the appropriate references, materials, and
equipment.

Standard: Per the appropriate references.

Concept of task: None.

Prerequisites: None.

CRP: 0   **Sustainment Interval (months):** 0

External Support Required: None.

Events updated: None.

Reference(s): MCO P1040R.35, Reserve Career Planning and Retention
Manual
MCO P1040.31, Enlisted Career Planning and Retention
Manual

Event code: 166-CPC

Task: Identify the key terms and definitions pertaining to Career
Planning.

Condition: Provided with the appropriate references, materials, and
equipment.

Standard: Per the appropriate references.

Concept of task: None.

Prerequisites: None.

CRP: 0   **Sustainment Interval (months):** 0

External Support Required: None.

Events updated: None.

Reference(s): MCO P1040R.35, Reserve Career Planning and Retention
Manual
MCO P1040.31, Enlisted Career Planning and Retention
Manual

Event code: 167-CPC

Task: Explain the FTAP interview.

Condition: Provided with the appropriate references, materials, and
E-26   equipment

Standard: Per the appropriate references.

Concept of task: None.

Prerequisites: None.

CRP: 0 **Sustainment Interval (months):** 0

External Support Required: None.

Events updated: None.

Reference(s): MCO P1040R.35, Reserve Career Planning and Retention
Manual
MCO P1040.31, Enlisted Career Planning and Retention
Manual

Event code: 168-CPC

Task: Explain the EAS interview.

Condition: Provided with the appropriate references, materials, and
equipment.

Standard: MCO P1040.31, Enlisted Career Planning and Retention Manual.

Concept of task: None.

Prerequisites: None.

CRP: 0 **Sustainment Interval (months):** 0

External Support Required: None.

Events updated: None.

Reference(s): MCO P1040.31, Enlisted Career Planning and Retention
Manual

Event code: 169-CPC

Task: Explain unscheduled interviews.

Condition: provided with the appropriate references, materials, and
equipment.

Standard: Per the appropriate references.

Concept of task: None.

Prerequisites: None.

CRP: 0 **Sustainment Interval (months):** 0

External Support Required: None.

Events updated: None.

Reference(s): MCO P1040R.35, Reserve Career Planning and Retention Manual
MCO P1040.31, Enlisted Career Planning and Retention Manual

Event code: 170-CPC

Task: Calculate the SRBP.

Condition: Provided with the appropriate references, materials, and utilizing the Marine Corps Opportunities Book (Career Planner Edition)(MCOB-CP).

Standard: MCO 7220.24, Selective Reenlistment Bonus Program (SRBP).

Concept of task: None.

Prerequisites: None.

CRP: 0 **Sustainment Interval (months):** 0

External Support Required: None.

Events updated: None.

Reference(s): MCO 7220.24, Selective Reenlistment Bonus Program (SRBP)

Event code: 171-CPR

Task: Explain a three month interview.

Condition: Provided with the appropriate references, materials, and equipment.

Standard: MCO P1040R.35, Reserve Career Planning and Retention Manual.

Concept of task: None.

Prerequisites: None.

CRP: 0 **Sustainment Interval (months):** 0

External Support Required: None.

Events updated: None.

Reference(s): MCO P1040R.35, Reserve Career Planning and Retention Manual

Event code: 172-CPC

Task: Explain the procedures for completing a waiver of reenlistment prerequisites.

Condition: Provided with the appropriate references, materials, and equipment.

Standard: MCO P1040.31, Enlisted Career Planning and Retention Manual.

Concept of task: None.

Prerequisites: None.

CRP: 0 **Sustainment Interval (months):** 0

External Support Required: None.

Events updated: None.

CHAPTER 1

Reference(s): MCO P1040.31, Enlisted Career Planning and Retention Manual

Event code: 173-CPC

Task: Complete a request for waiver of reenlistment prerequisites.

Condition: Provided with the appropriate references, materials, and equipment.

Standard: MCO P1040.31, Enlisted Career Planning and Retention Manual.

Concept of task: None.

Prerequisites: None.

CRP: 0   **Sustainment Interval (months):** 0

External Support Required: None.

Events updated: None.

Reference(s): MCO P1040.31, Enlisted Career Planning and Retention Manual

Event code: 174-CPC

Task: Explain the procedures for completing naval correspondence.

Condition: Provided with the appropriate references, materials, and equipment.

Standard: SECNAVINST 5216.5, Correspondence Manual.

Concept of task: None.

Prerequisites: None.

CRP: 0   **Sustainment Interval (months):** 0

External Support Required: None.

Events updated: None.

Reference(s): SECNAVINST 5216.5, Correspondence Manual

Event code: 175-CPC

Task: Explain the responsibility and procedures between parent and host command regarding FAP and TAD Marines

Condition: Provided with the appropriate references, materials, and equipment.

Standard: Per the appropriate references.

Concept of task: None.

Prerequisites: None.

CRP: 0   **Sustainment Interval (months):** 0

External Support Required: None.

Events updated: None.

Reference(s): MCO P1040R.35, Reserve Career Planning and Retention
Manual
MCO P1040.31, Enlisted Career planning and Retention
Manual

Event code: 176-CPC

Task: Explain the required SRH entries as it pertains to Career Planning.

Condition: provided with the appropriate references, materials, and
Equipment.

Standard: Per the appropriate references.

Concept of task: None.

Prerequisites: None.

CRP: 0 **Sustainment Interval (months)**: 0

External Support Required: None.

Events updated: None.

Reference(s): MCO P1070.12, Marine Corps Individual Records
Administration Manual (IRAM)
MCO P1001R.1, Marine Corps Reserve Administration
Management Manual (MCRAMM)

Event code: 177-CPC

Task: Explain the boat space report.

Condition: Provided with the appropriate references, materials, and
Equipment

Standard: MCO P1040.31, Enlisted Career Planning and Retention Manual.

Concept of task: None.

Prerequisites: None.

CRP: 0 **Sustainment Interval (months)**: 0

External Support Required: None.

Events updated: None.

Reference(s): MCO P1040.31, Enlisted Career Planning and Retention
Manual

Event code: 178-CPC

Task: Explain applicable codes as they pertain to Career Planning.

Condition: Provided with the appropriate references, materials, and
equipment.

E-30

Standard: MCO P1080.20, Marine Corps Total Force Codes Manual
(MCTFSCODESMAN).

Concept of task: None.

Prerequisites: None.

CRP: 0 **Sustainment Interval (months):** 0

External Support Required: None.

Events updated: None.

Reference(s): MCO P1080.20, Marine Corps Total Force Codes Manual
(MCTFSCODESMAN)

Event code: 179-CPC

Task: Explain the purposes for extension.

Condition: Provided with the appropriate references, materials, and
equipment.

Standard: Per the appropriate references.

Concept of task: None.

Prerequisites: None.

CRP: 0 **Sustainment Interval (months):** 0

External Support Required: None.

Events updated: None.

Reference(s): MCO P1040R.35, Reserve Career Planning and Retention
Manual
MCO P1040.31, Enlisted Career Planning and Retention
Manual

Event code: 180-CPR

Task: Explain the required six month interview.

Condition: Provided with the appropriate references, materials, and
equipment.

Standard: MCO P1040R.35, Reserve Career Planning and Retention Manual.

Concept of task: None.

Prerequisites: None.

CRP: 0 **Sustainment Interval (months):** 0

External Support Required: None.

Events updated: None.

Reference(s): MCO P1040R.35, Reserve Career Planning and Retention Manual

Event code: 181-CPR

Task: Explain the Reserve Sponsorship Program.

Condition: Provided with the appropriate references, materials, and equipment.

Standard: MCO P1040R.35, Reserve Career Planning and Retention Manual.

Concept of task: None.

Prerequisites: None.

CRP: 0 **Sustainment Interval (months):** 0

External Support Required: None.

Events updated: None.

Reference(s): MCO P1040R.35, Reserve Career Planning and Retention Manual

Event code: 182-CPR

Task: Explain the Training Pay Category P Program (CAT P)

Condition: Provided with the appropriate references, materials, and equipment.

Standard: MCO 1500R.36, Training/Category P Program.

Concept of task: None.

Prerequisites: None.

CRP: 0 **Sustainment Interval (months):** 0

External Support Required: None.

Events updated: None.

Reference(s): MCO 1500R.36, Training/Category P Program

Event code: 183-CPR

Task: Explain on contract waivers of reenlistment prerequisites.

Condition: Provided with the appropriate references, materials, and equipment.

Standard: MCO P1040R.35, Reserve Career Planning and Retention Manual.

Concept of task: None.

Prerequisites: None.

CRP: 0 **Sustainment Interval (months):** 0

External Support Required: None.

Events updated: None.

Reference(s): MCO P1040R.35, Reserve Career Planning and Retention Manual
E-32

CHAPTER 1

Event code: 184-CPR

Task: Explain the Selected Reserve Incentive Programs.

Condition: Provided with the appropriate references, materials, and utilizing the Marine Corps Opportunities Book (Career Planner Edition) (MCOB-CP).

Standard: MCO 7220R.38, Selective Reserve Incentive Program.

Concept of task: None.

Prerequisites: None.

CRP: 0 **Sustainment Interval (months):** 0

External Support Required: None.

Events updated: None.

Reference(s): MCO 7220R.38, Selective Reserve Incentive Program

Event code: 185-CPR

Task: Explain the Reserve Career options.

Condition: Provided with the appropriate references, materials, and utilizing the Marine Corps Opportunities Book (Career Planner Edition) (MCOB-CP).

Standard: MCO P1040R.35, Reserve Career Planning and Retention Manual.

Concept of task: None.

Prerequisites: None.

CRP: 0 **Sustainment Interval (months):** 0

External Support Required: None.

Events updated: None.

Reference(s): MCO P1040R.35, Reserve Career Planning and Retention Manual

Event code: 186-CPC

Task: Produce a Career Planning product in the current Marine Corps presentation software application.

Condition: Provided with the appropriate references, materials, and equipment.

Standard: Per the appropriate software users manuals.

Concept of task: None.

Prerequisites: None.

CRP: 0 **Sustainment Interval (months):** 0

External Support Required: None.

Events updated: None.

Reference(s): Per the appropriate software users manuals

Event code: 187-CPC

Task: Produce a Career Planning product in the current Marine Corps database software application.

Condition: Provided with the appropriate references, materials, and equipment.

Standard: Per the appropriate software users manuals.

Concept of task: None.

Prerequisites: None.

CRP: 0   **Sustainment Interval (months):** 0

External Support Required: None.

Events updated: None.

Reference(s): Per the appropriate software users manuals

Event code: 188-CPC

Task: Produce a Career Planning product in the current Marine Corps word processing software application.

Condition: Provided with the appropriate references, materials, and equipment.

Standard: Per the appropriate software users manuals.

Concept of task: None.

Prerequisites: None.

CRP: 0   **Sustainment Interval (months):** 0

External Support Required: None.

Events updated: None.

Reference(s): Per the appropriate software users manuals

Event code: 189-CPC

Task: Produce a Career Planning product in the current Marine Corps spreadsheet software application.

Condition: Provided with the appropriate references, materials, and equipment.

Standard: Per the appropriate software users manuals.

Concept of task: None.

Prerequisites: None.

CRP: 0   **Sustainment Interval (months):** 0

E-34

External Support Required: None.

Events updated: None.

Reference(s): Per the appropriate software users manuals

Event code: 190-CPC

Task: Locate online sources of Career Planning information.

Condition: Provided with the appropriate references, materials, and equipment.

Standard: Per the appropriate references.

Concept of task: None.

Prerequisites: None.

CRP: 0   **Sustainment Interval (months):** 0

External Support Required: None.

Events updated: None.

Reference(s): Per the appropriate software users manuals

Event code: 191-CPC

Task: Identify on-line sources of Career Planning information.

Condition: Provided with the appropriate references, materials, and equipment.

Standard: Per the appropriate references.

Concept of task: None.

Prerequisites: None.

CRP: 0   **Sustainment Interval (months):** 0

External Support Required: None.

Events updated: None.

Reference(s): Per the appropriate software users manuals

Event code: 192-CPC

Task: Explain the elements which a Career Planner may choose from in the creation of desktop procedures.

Condition: Provided with the appropriate references, materials, and equipment.

Standard: Per the appropriate references.

Concept of task: None.

Prerequisites: None.

CRP: 0   **Sustainment Interval (months):** 0

External Support Required: None.

Events updated: None.

Reference(s): MCO P1040R.35, Reserve Career Planning and Retention Manual
MCO P1040.31, Enlisted Career Planning and Retention Manual

Event code: 193-CPC

Task: Explain the Survivors Benefit Program.

Condition: Provided with the appropriate references, materials, and utilizing the Marine Corps Opportunities Book (Career Planner Edition)(MCOB-CP).

Standard: MCO P1741.11, Survivor Benefit Plan.

Concept of task: None.

Prerequisites: None.

CRP: 0   **Sustainment Interval (months)**: 0

External Support Required: None.

Events updated: None.

Reference(s): MCO P1741.11, Survivor Benefit Plan

Event code: 194-CPC

Task: Explain the contact to contract process.

Condition: Provided with the appropriate references, materials, and equipment.

Standard: Per the appropriate references.

Concept of task: None.

Prerequisites: None.

CRP: 0   **Sustainment Interval (months)**: 0

External Support Required: None.

Events updated: None.

Reference(s): MCO P1040.31, Enlisted Career Planning and Retention Manual
MCO P1040R.35, Reserve Career Planning and Retention Manual

CHAPTER 1

APPENDIX F

COMBAT READY TRAINING (200 LEVEL)

Purpose: The 200 level of training is centered around formal schools and Managed On-the-Job Training (MOJT) and requires the career planner to apply the elements of Systematic Career Planning. The transition from 200 level training to 300 level training is marked by the attendance of the Advanced Career Planner Course (ACPC)

Administrative Notes: None.

Prerequisites: None.

Event code: 200-CPC

Task: Process a RELM.

Condition: Provided with the appropriate references, materials, and equipment.

Standard: Per the appropriate references.

Concept of task: None.

Prerequisites: None.

CRP: 0.81 **Sustainment Interval (months):** .5

External Support Required: None.

Events updated: None.

Reference(s): MCO P1040R.3S, Reserve Career Planning and Retention Manual
MCO P1040.31, Enlisted Career Planning and Retention Manual

Event code: 201-CPC

Task: Conduct initial interviews.

Condition: Provided with the appropriate references, materials, and utilizing the Marine Corps Opportunities Book (Career Planner Edition) (MCOB-CP).

Standard: Per the appropriate references.

Concept of task: None.

Prerequisites: None.

CRP: 0.81 **Sustainment Interval (months):** 1

External Support Required: None.

Events updated: None.

Reference(s): MCO P1040R.35, Reserve Career Planning and Retention Manual
MCO P1040.31, Enlisted Career Planning and Retention Manual

Event code: 202-CPC

Task: Conduct FTAP interviews.

Condition: Provided with the appropriate references, materials, and utilizing the Marine Corps Opportunities Book (Career Planner Edition)(MCOB-CP).

Standard: Per the appropriate references.

Concept of task: None.

Prerequisites: None.

CRP: 0.81 **Sustainment Interval (months):** 12

External Support Required: None.

Events updated: None.

Reference(s): MCO P1040R.35, Reserve Career Planning and Retention Manual

MCO P1040.31, Enlisted Career Planning and Retention Manual

Event code: 203-CPC

Task: Conduct EAS interviews.

Condition: provided with the appropriate references, materials, and utilizing the Marine Corps Opportunities Book (Career Planner Edition) (MCOB-CP).

Standard: MCO P1040.31, Enlisted Career Planning and Retention Manual.

Concept of task: None.

Prerequisites: None.

CRP: 0.81 **Sustainment Interval (months):** 3

External Support Required: None.

Events updated: None.

Reference(s): MCO P1040.31, Enlisted Career Planning and Retention Manual

Event code: 204-CPR

Task: Conduct a six month interview.

Condition: Provided with the appropriate references, materials, and utilizing the Marine Corps Opportunities Book (Career Planner Edition)(MCOB-CP).

Standard: MCO P1040R.35, Reserve Career Planning and Retention Manual.

Concept of task: None.

Prerequisites: None.

CRP: 0.81 **Sustainment Interval (months):** 3

External Support Required: None.

Events updated: None.

Reference(s): MCO P1040R.35, Reserve Career Planning and Retention Manual

Event code: 205-CPC

Task: Conduct Area Canvassing (AC).

Condition: Provided with the. appropriate references, materials, and utilizing the Marine Corps Opportunities Book (Career Planner Edition) (MCOB-CP).

Standard: Achieve Global.

Concept of task: None.

Prerequisites: None.

CRP: 0.27 **Sustainment Interval (months):** 1

External Support Required: None.

Events updated: None.

Reference(s): Achieve Global products

Event code: 206-CPC

Task: Complete a Statement of Service (SOS)

Condition: Provided with the appropriate references, materials, and equipment.

Standard: Per the appropriate references.

Concept of task: None.

Prerequisites: None.

CRP: 0.27   **Sustainment Interval (months)**: 6

External Support Required: None.

Events updated: None.

Reference(s):   DOD Pay Entitlements Manual (DOD PM)
MCO P1080.20, Marine Corps Total Force Codes Manual (MCTFSCODESMAN)
MCO P1900.16, Marine Corps Separation and Retirement Manual (SEPMAN)
MCO 7220.31, Joint Uniform Military Pay System Field Procedures Manual

Event code: 207-CPC

Task: Submit a RELM.

Condition: Provided with the appropriate references, materials, and equipment.

Standard: Per the appropriate references.

Concept of task: None.

Prerequisites: None.

CRP: 0.54   **Sustainment Interval (months)**: .5

External Support Required: None.

Events updated: None.

Reference(s):   MCO P1040R.35, Reserve Career Planning and Retention Manual
MCO P1040.31, Enlisted Career Planning and Retention Manual

Event code: 208-CPC

Task: Explain educational opportunities.

Condition: Provided with the appropriate references, materials, and utilizing the Marine Corps Opportunities Book (Career Planner Edition)(MCOB-CP).

Standard: Per the appropriate references.

Concept of task: None.

Prerequisites: None.

CRP: 0.27 **Sustainment Interval (months):** 1

External Support Required: None.

Events updated: None.

Reference(s): MCO 1550.22, Marine Corps Apprenticeship Program
MCO 1550.23, Military Academic Skills Program (MASP)
MCO 1560.21, Degree Completion Program for Staff
Noncommissioned Officers
MCO 1560R.30, Selected Reserve Montgomery GI Bill (MGIB-R)
MCO 1560.24, Broadened Opportunity for Officer Selection
and Training Program (BOOST)
MCO 1560.28, Veterans Educational Assistance Program (VEAP)
MCO 1560.26, Marine Corps Tuition Assistance Program
OPNAVINST 1780.2, Montgomery GI Bill (NOTAL)

Event code: 209-CPC

Task: Explain Marine Corps benefits.

Condition: Provided with the appropriate references, materials, and
utilizing the Marine Corps Opportunities Book (Career Planner
Edition)(MCOB-CP)

Standard: Per the appropriate references.

Concept of task: None.

Prerequisites: None.

CRP: 0.54 **Sustainment Interval (months):** 1

External Support Required: None.

Events updated: None.

Reference(s): MCO 1560.15, Marine Corps Enlisted Commissioning Education
Program (MECEP)
MCO 1560.21, Degree Completion Program for Staff
Noncommissioned Officers
MCO P1040R.35, Reserve Career Planning and Retention Manual

Event code: 210-CPR

Task: Determine a Marine's Mandatory Drill Stop Date.

Condition: Provided with the appropriate references, materials, and
equipment.

Standard: MCO P1040R.35, Reserve Career Planning and Retention Manual.

Concept of task: None.

Prerequisites: None.

CRP: 0.54 **Sustainment Interval (months):** 12

External Support Required: None.

Events updated: None.

Reference(s): MCO P1040R.35, Reserve Career Planning and Retention Manual

Event code: 211-CPC

Task: Calculate pay and allowances as it pertains to Career Planning.

Condition: Provided with the appropriate references, materials, and equipment.

Standard: Per the appropriate references.

Concept of task: None.

Prerequisites: None.

CRP: 0.27 **Sustainment Interval (months):** 12

External Support Required: None.

Events updated: None.

Reference(s): Department of Defense Financial Management Regulation (DODFMR)
MCO 7220.31, Joint Uniform Military Pay System Field Procedures Manual

Event code: 212-CPC

Task: Calculate Lump Sum Leave (LSL).

Condition: Provided with the appropriate references, materials, and equipment.

Standard: Per the appropriate references.

Concept of task: None.

Prerequisites: None.

CRP: 0.54 **Sustainment Interval (months):** 3

External Support Required: None.

Events updated: None.

Reference(s): Department of Defense Financial Management Regulation (DODFMR)
MCO P1050.3, Leave and Liberty Manual
MCO 7220.31, Joint Uniform Military Pay System Field Procedures Manual

Event code: 213-CPC

Task: Navigate in Marine Corps Total Forces system (MCTFS).

Condition: Provided with the appropriate references, materials, and equipment.

Standard: Per the appropriate references.

Concept of task: None.

Prerequisites: None.

CRP: 0.27 **Sustainment Interval (months):** .5

External Support Required: None.

Events updated: None.

Reference(s): MCO P1040R.35, Reserve Career Planning and Retention Manual
MCO P1040.31, Enlisted Career Planning and Retention Manual

Event code: 214-CPC

Task: Explain the Overseas Extension Process System (OEPS).

Condition: Provided with the appropriate references, materials, and utilizing the Marine Corps Opportunities Book (Career Planner Edition)(MCOB-CP).

Standard: Per the appropriate references.

Concept of task: None.

Prerequisites: None.

CRP: 0.27 **Sustainment Interval (months):** 3

External Support Required: None.

Events updated: None.

Reference(s): MCO P1070.12, Marine Corps Individual Records Administration Manual (IRAM)

Event code: 215-CPC

Task: Complete an agreement to extend enlistment form (NAVMC 321a).

Condition: Provided with the appropriate references, materials, and equipment.

Standard: Per the appropriate references.

Concept of task: None.

Prerequisites: None.

CRP: 0.81 **Sustainment Interval (months):** 1

External Support Required: None.

Events updated: None.

Reference(s): MCO P1070.12, Marine Corps Individual Records Administration Manual (IRAM)
MCO P1001R.1, Marine Corps Reserve Administration Management Manual (MCRAMM)

Event code: 216-CPC

Task: Complete a reenlistment contract (DD Form 4)

Condition: Provided with the appropriate references, materials, and equipment

Standard: Per the appropriate references.

Concept of task: None.

Prerequisites: None.

CRP: 0.81 **Sustainment Interval (months):** 1

External Support Required: None.

Events updated: None.

Reference(s): MCO P1070.12, Marine Corps Individual Records Administration Manual (IRAM)
MCO P1001R.1, Marine Corps Reserve Administration Management Manual (MCRAMM)

Event code: 217-CPC

Task: Conduct a reenlistment ceremony.

Condition: Provided with the appropriate references, materials, and equipment.

Standard: Per the appropriate references.

Concept of task: None.

Prerequisites: None.

CRP: 0.54 **Sustainment Interval (months):** 1

External Support Required: None.

Events updated: None.

Reference(s): MCO P1040R.35, Reserve Career Planning and Retention Manual
MCO P1040.31, Enlisted Career Planning and Retention Manual

Event code: 21B-CPC

Task: Complete required reenlistment certificates.

Condition: Provided with the appropriate references, materials, and equipment.

Standard: Per the appropriate references.

Concept of task: None.

Prerequisites: None.

CRP: 0.54 **Sustainment Interval (months):** 1

External Support Required: None.

Events updated: None.

Reference(s): MCO P1040.31, Enlisted Career Planning and Retention Manual
MCO P1040R.35, Reserve Career Planning and Retention Manual

CHAPTER 1
MCO P1900.16, Marine Corps Separation and Retirement Manual
(SEPMAN)

Event code: 219-CPC

Task: Submit RELM for separation pay determination.

Condition: provided with the appropriate references, materials, and equipment.

Standard: Per the appropriate references.

Concept of task: None.

Prerequisites: None.

CRP: 0.54 **Sustainment Interval (months):** 12

External Support Required: None.

Events updated: None.

Reference(s): MCO P1040.31, Enlisted Career Planning and Retention Manual
MCO P1040R.35, Reserve Career Planning and Retention Manual
MCO P1900.16, Marine Corps Separation and Retirement Manual
(SEPMAN)

Event code: 220-CPR

Task: Manage the Reserve Referral Credit Program.

Condition: Provided with the appropriate references, materials, and equipment.

Standard: Per the appropriate references.

Concept of task: None.

Prerequisites: None.

CRP: 0.81 **Sustainment Interval (months):** 1

External Support Required: None.

Events updated: None.

Reference(s): MCO 1130.56, Total Force Recruiting
MCO P1040R.35, Reserve Career Planning and Retention Manual

Event code: 221-CPC

Task: Provide guidance on enlisted to officer programs.

Condition: Provided with the appropriate references, materials, and utilizing the Marine Corps Opportunities Book (Career Planner Edition)(MCOB-CP).

Standard: Per the appropriate references.

Concept of task: None.

Prerequisites: None.

CRP: 0.27 Sustainment Interval (months) 3

External Support Required: None.

Events updated: None.

Reference(s): MCO 1560.15, Marine Corps Enlisted Commissioning Education Program (MECEP)
MCO 1560.21, Degree Completion Program for Staff Noncommissioned Officers
MCO 1560.24, Broadened Opportunity for Officer Selection and Training Program (BOOST)
MCO 1530.11, Naval Academy/Naval Preparatory School
MCO 1040.42, Marine Corps Limited Duty Officer/Warrant Officer (LDO/WO) Program
MCO 1040.43, Enlisted to Officer Commissioning Program (ECP/MCP)
MCO 1040R.10, Selected Marine Corps Reserve Direct Commissioning (SMCRDC) Program

Event code: 222-CPC

Task: Process special duty assignment packages.

Condition: Provided with the appropriate references, materials, and equipment.

Standard: MCO P1326.6, SDA Manual.

Concept of task: None.

Prerequisites: None.

CRP: 0.81 **Sustainment Interval (months):** 3

External Support Required: None.

Events updated: None.

Reference(s): MCO P1326.6, SDA Manual

Event code: 223-CPC

Task: Complete an AA Form.

Condition: Provided with the appropriate references, materials, and equipment.

Standard: SECNAVINST 5216.5, Correspondence Manual.

Concept of task: None.

Prerequisites: None.

CRP: 0.27 **Sustainment Interval (months):** 12

External Support Required: None.

Events updated: None.

Reference(s): SECNAVINST 5216.5, Correspondence Manual

Event code: 224-CPC

Task: Draft a Naval message.

Condition: Provided with the appropriate references, materials, and equipment.

Standard: SECNAVINST 5216.5, Correspondence Manual.

Concept of task: None.

Prerequisites: None.

CRP: 0.54 **Sustainment Interval (months):** 3

External Support Required: None.

Events updated: None.

Reference(s): SECNAVINST 5216.5, Correspondence Manual

Event code: 225-CPC

Task: Explain the Quality Reenlistment Program (QRP)

Condition: provided with the appropriate references, materials, and equipment.

Standard: SECNAVINST 5216.5, Correspondence Manual.

Concept of task: None.

Prerequisites: None.

CRP: 0.27 **Sustainment Interval (months):** 12

External Support Required: None.

Events updated: None.

Reference(s): SECNAVINST 5216.5, Correspondence Manual

Event code: 226-CPC

Task: Maintain the Career Planning Contact Record.

Condition: Provided with the appropriate references, materials, and equipment.

Standard: Per the appropriate references.

Concept of task: None.

Prerequisites: None.

CRP: 0.81 **Sustainment Interval (months):** 1

External Support Required: None.

Events updated: None.

Reference(s): MCO P1040.31, Enlisted Career Planning and Retention Manual
MCO P1040R.35, Reserve Career Planning and Retention Manual

Event code: 227-CPC

Task: Calculate the SRBP.

Condition: Provided with the appropriate references, materials, and equipment.

Standard: MCO 7220.24, Selective Reenlistment Bonus Program (SRBP).

Concept of task: None.

Prerequisites: None.

CRP: 0.54 **Sustainment Interval (months)**: 3

External Support Required: None.

Events updated: None.

Reference(s): MCO 7220.24, Selective Reenlistment Bonus Programs(SRBP)

Event code: 228-CPC

Task: Complete a request for waiver of reenlistment perquisites.

Condition: Provided with the appropriate references, materials, and equipment.

Standard: MCO P1040.31, Enlisted Career Planning and Retention Manual.

Concept of task: None.

Prerequisites: None.

CRP: 0.54 **Sustainment Interval (months)**: 3

External Support Required: None.

Events updated: None.

Reference(s): MCO P1040.31, Enlisted Career Planning and Retention Manual

Event code: 229-CPC

Task: Coordinate with other units in Career Planning matters as they pertain to FAP/TAD Marines.

Condition: Provided with the appropriate references, materials, and equipment.

Standard: Per the appropriate references.

Concept of task: None.

Prerequisites: None.

CRP: 0.27 **Sustainment Interval (months)**: 12

External Support Required: None.

Events updated: None.

Reference(s): MCO P1040.31, Enlisted Career Planning and Retention Manual
MCO P1040R.35, Reserve Career Planning and Retention Manual
Local SOP

Event code: 230-CPC

Task: Complete required SRB entries.

Condition: Provided with the appropriate references, materials, and Equipment

Standard: Per the appropriate references.

Concept of task: None.

Prerequisites: None.

CRP: 0.27 **Sustainment Interval (months):** 3

External Support Required: None.

Events updated: None.

Reference(s): MCO P1001R.1, Marine Corps Reserve Administration Management Manual (MCRAMM)
MCO P1070.12, Marine Corps Individual Records Administration Manual (IRAM)

Event code: 231-CPR

Task: Manage the Reserve Sponsorship Program.

Condition: Provided with the appropriate references, materials, and equipment.

Standard: MCO P1040R.35, Reserve Career Planning and Retention Manual.

Concept of task: None.

Prerequisites: None.

CRP: 0.54 **Sustainment Interval (months):** 6

External Support Required: None.

Events updated: None.

Reference(s): MCO P1040R.35, Reserve Career Planning and Retention Manual

Event code: 232-CPR

Task: Manage the CAT-P Program.

Condition: Provided with the appropriate references, materials, and equipment.

Standard: Per the appropriate references.

Concept of task: None.

Prerequisites: None.

CRP: 0.27 **Sustainment Interval (months):** 12

External Support Required: None.

Events updated: None.

Reference(s): MCO P1040R.35, Reserve Career Planning and Retention Manual
MCO 1500R.36, Training/Category P Program

Event code: 233-CPR

Task: Complete an on-contract waiver of reenlistment prerequisites.

Condition: Provided with the appropriate references, materials, and equipment.

Standard: MCO P1040R.35, Reserve Career Planning and Retention Manual.

Concept of task: None.

Prerequisites: None.

CRP: 0.54 **Sustainment Interval (months):** 12

External Support Required: None.

Events updated: None.

Reference(s): MCO P1040R.35, Reserve Career Planning and Retention Manual

Event code: 234-CPR

Task: Explain the Selected Reserve Incentive Programs.

Condition: Provided with the appropriate references, materials, and utilizing the Marine Corps Opportunities Book (Career Planner Edition) (MCOB-CP)

Standard: MCO 7220R.38, Selected Reserve Incentive Programs.

Concept of task: None.

Prerequisites: None.

CRP: 0.54 **Sustainment Interval (months):** 3

External Support Required: None.

Events updated: None.

Reference(s): MCO 7220R.38, Selected Reserve Incentive Programs

Event code: 235-CPC

Task: Explain the Reserve Career options.

Condition: Provided with the appropriate references, materials, and utilizing the Marine Corps Opportunities Book (Career Planner Edition)(MCOB-CP).

Standard: MCO P1040R.35, Reserve Career Planning and Retention Manual.

Concept of task: None.

Prerequisites: None.

CRP: 0.54 **Sustainment Interval (months):** 3

External Support Required: None.

Events updated: None.

Reference(s): MCO P1040R.35, Reserve Career Planning and Retention Manual

Event code: 236-CPC

Task: Complete a Career Planners report.

Condition: Provided with the appropriate references, materials, and equipment.

Standard: Local SOP.

Concept of task: None.

Prerequisites: None.

CRP: 0.81 **Sustainment Interval (months):** 1

External Support Required: None.

Events updated: None.

Reference(s): Local SOP

Event code: 237-CPC

Task: Prepare Career Planning related product in the current Marine Corps presentation application.

Condition: Provided with the appropriate references, materials, and equipment.

Standard: Per the appropriate software users manuals.

Concept of task: None.

Prerequisites: None.

CRP: 0.54 **Sustainment Interval (months):** 3

External Support Required: None.

Events updated: None.

Reference(s): Per the appropriate software users manuals

Event code: 238-CPC

Task: Maintain the Individual Case file.

Condition: Provided with the appropriate references, materials, and equipment.

Standard: Per the appropriate references.

Concept of task: None.

Prerequisites: None.

CRP: 0.81 **Sustainment Interval (months):** 1

External Support Required: None.

Events updated: None.

Reference(s): MCO P1040.31, Enlisted Career Planning and Retention Manual
MCO P1040R.35, Reserve Career Planning and Retention Manual

Event code: 239-CPC

Task: Identify Marines requiring interviews.

Condition: Provided with the appropriate references, materials, and equipment.

Standard: Per the appropriate references.

Concept of task: None.

Prerequisites: None.

CRP: 0.81 **Sustainment Interval (months):** .5

External Support Required: None.

Events updated: None.

Reference(s): MCO P1040.31, Enlisted Career planning and Retention Manual
MCO P1040R.35, Reserve Career Planning and Retention Manual

Event code: 240-CPC

Task: Analyze Career Planning data.

Condition: Provided with the appropriate references, materials, and equipment.

Standard: Per the appropriate references.

Concept of task: None.

Prerequisites: None.

CRP: 0.81 **Sustainment Interval (months):** 1

External Support Required: None.

Events updated: None.

Reference(s): MCO P1040.31, Enlisted Career Planning and Retention Manual
MCO P1040R.35, Reserve Career Planning and Retention Manual

Event code: 241-CPC

Task: Forward associated reenlistment/extension documents, as required.

Condition: provided with the appropriate references, materials, and equipment.

Standard: Per the appropriate references.

Concept of task: None.

Prerequisites: None.

CRP: 0.54 **Sustainment Interval (months):** 1

External Support Required: None.

Events updated: None.

Reference(s): MCO P1040.31, Enlisted Career Planning and Retention Manual

Event code: 245-CPC

Task: Prepare Career Planning related product in the current Marine Corps database application.

Condition: Provided with the appropriate references, materials, and equipment.

Standard: Per the appropriate software users manuals.

Concept of task: None.

Prerequisites: None.

CRP: 0.27 **Sustainment Interval (months):** 3

External Support Required: None.

Events updated: None.

Reference(s): Per the appropriate software users manuals

Event code: 246-CPC

Task: Prepare Career Planning related product in the current Marine Corps word processing application.

Condition: Provided with the appropriate references, materials, and equipment.

Standard: Per the appropriate software users manuals.

Concept of task: None.

Prerequisites: None.

CRP: 0.27 **Sustainment Interval (months):** 1

External Support Required: None.

Events updated: None.

Reference(s): Per the appropriate software users manuals

Event code: 247-CPC

Task: Prepare Career Planning related product in the Current Marine Corps spreadsheet application.

Condition: Provided with the appropriate references, materials, and equipment.

Standard: Per the appropriate software users manuals.

Concept of task: None.

Prerequisites: None.

CRP: 0.27 **Sustainment Interval (months):** 1

External Support Required: None.

Events updated: None.

Reference(s): Per the appropriate software users manuals

Event code: 248-CPC

Task: Execute FTAP within your command.

Condition: Provided with the appropriate references, materials, and equipment.

Standard: Local SOP.

Concept of task: None.

Prerequisites: None.

CRP: 0.81 **Sustainment Interval (months):** 1

External Support Required: None.

Events updated: None.

Reference(s): Local SOP

Event code: 249-CPR

Task: Conduct a three month interview.

Condition: Provided with the appropriate references, materials, and utilizing the Marine Corps Opportunities Book (Career Planner Edition) (MCOB-CP)

Standard: MCO P1040R.35, Reserve Career Planning and Retention Manual.

Concept of task: None.

Prerequisites: None.

CRP: 0.81 **Sustainment Interval (months):** 3

External Support Required: None.

Events updated: None.

Reference(s): MCO P1040R.35, Reserve Career Planning and Retention Manual

Event code: 250-CPC

Task: Maintain desktop procedures.

Condition: Provided with the appropriate references, materials, and equipment.

Standard: Per the appropriate references.

Concept of task: None.

Prerequisites: None.

CRP: 0.27 **Sustainment Interval (months):** 3

External Support Required: None.

Events updated: None.

Reference(s): MCO P1040.31, Enlisted Career Planning and Retention Manual
MCO P1040R.35, Reserve Career Planning and Retention Manual

Local SOP

Event code: 251-CPC

Task: Brief Marines on the Survivors Benefit Program.

Condition: Provided with the appropriate references, materials, and utilizing the Marine Corps Opportunities Book (Career Planner Edition) (MCOB-CP).

Standard: MCO P1741.11, Survivor Benefit Plan.

Concept of task: None.

Prerequisites: None.

CRP: 0.27 **Sustainment Interval (months):** 6

External Support Required: None.

Events updated: None.

Reference(s): MCO P1741.11, Survivor Benefit Plan

Event code: 252-CPC

Task: Apply the systematic approach to Career Planning.

Condition: Provided with the appropriate references, materials, and equipment.

Standard: Per the appropriate references.

Concept of task: None.

Prerequisites: None

CRP: 0.81 **Sustainment Interval (months):** .5

External Support Required: None

Events updated: None

Reference(s): MCO P1040.31, Enlisted Career Planning and Retention Manual
MCO P1040R.35, Reserve Career Planning and Retention Manual

Event code: 253-CPC

Task: Apply the contact to contract process.

Condition: Provided with the appropriate references, materials, and equipment.

Standard: Per the appropriate references.

Concept of task: None.

Prerequisites: None

CRP: 0.81 **Sustainment Interval (months):** .5

External Support Required: None

Events updated: None

Reference(s): MCO P1040.31, Enlisted Career Planning and Retention Manual
MCO P1040R.35, Reserve Career Planning and Retention Manual

CHAPTER 1

APPENDIX G

COMBAT QUALIFICATION TRAINING (300 LEVEL)

Purpose: The transition from 200 level training to 300 level training is marked by the attendance of the Advanced Career Planner Course (ACPC). ACPC is conducted at MCRD San Diego, CA and provides instruction in the advanced components of Systematic Career Planning; mentoring and development. Upon graduation of ACPC the Marine will enter the 300 level of training. The 300 level of training is centered around formal schools and MOJT. During the 300 level of training the Marine will mentor, develop, and supervise Career Planners in their application of Systematic Career Planning.

Administrative Notes: None.

Prerequisites: None.

Event code: 300-CPA

Task: Implement a training plan for subordinates.

Condition: Provided with the appropriate references, materials, and equipment.

Standard: Career Planners Training and Readiness Manual.

Concept of task: None.

Prerequisites: None.

CRP: 0.54 **Sustainment Interval (months):**

External Support Required: None.

Events updated: None.

Reference(s): Career Planners Training and Readiness Manual Local SOP

Event code: 301-CPA

Task: Produce a Career Planner SOP.

Condition: Provided with the appropriate references, materials, and equipment.

Standard: Local SOP.

Concept of task: None.

Prerequisites: None.

CRP: 0.81 **Sustainment Interval (months):**

External Support Required: None.

Events updated: None.

Reference(s): Local SOP

Event code: 302-CPA

Task: Write a position paper.

Condition: Provided with the appropriate references, materials, and equipment.

Standard: Per the appropriate references.

Concept of task: None.

Prerequisites: None.

CRP: 0.27 **Sustainment Interval (months):**

External Support Required: None.

Events updated: None.

Reference(s): Local SOP
Joint Staff and Officers Guide
SECNAVINST 5216.5, Correspondence Manual

Event code: 303-CPA

Task: Develop a Retention Campaign Plan.

Condition: Provided with the appropriate references, materials, and equipment.

Standard: Local SOP.

Concept of task: None.

Prerequisites: None.

CRP: 0.54 **Sustainment Interval (months):**

External Support Required: None.

Events updated: None.

Reference(s): Local SOP

Event code: 304-CPA

Task: Conduct readiness inspections of subordinate commands.

Condition: Provided with the appropriate references, materials, and equipment.

Standard: Local SOP.

Concept of task: None.

Prerequisites: None.

CRP: 0.27 **Sustainment Interval (months):**

External Support Required: None.

Events updated: None.

Reference(s): Local SOP

Event code: 305-CPA

Task: Analyze Career Planning data.

Condition: Provided with the appropriate references, materials, and equipment.

Standard: Per the appropriate references.

Concept of task: None.

Prerequisites: None.

CRP: 0.27 **Sustainment Interval (months):**

External Support Required: None.

Events updated: None.

Reference(s): MCO P1040.31, Enlisted Career Planning and Retention Manual
MCO P1040R.35, Reserve Career Planning and Retention Manual

Local SOP

Event code: 306-CPA

Task: Analyze Career Planner's interview techniques.

Condition: Provided with the appropriate references, materials, and equipment.

Standard: Per the appropriate references.

Concept of task: None.

Prerequisites: None.

CRP: 0.27 **Sustainment Interval (months):**

External Support Required: None.

Events updated: None.

Reference(s): MCO P1040.31, Enlisted Career Planning and Retention Manual
MCO P1040R.35, Reserve Career Planning and Retention Manual
Local SOP

Event code: 307-CPA

Task: Observe Career Planner's interview techniques.

Condition: Provided with the appropriate references, materials, and Equipment

Standard: Local SOP.

Concept of task: None.

Prerequisites: None.

CRP: 0.81 **Sustainment Interval (months):**

External Support Required: None.

Events updated: None.

Reference(s): Local sop

Event code: 305-CPA

Task: Develop supportive Career Planning interview techniques.

Condition: Provided with the appropriate references, materials, and equipment.

Standard: Local SOP.

Concept of task: None.

Prerequisites: None.

CRP: 0.81 **Sustainment Interval (months):**

External Support Required: None.

Events updated: None.

Reference(s): Local SOP

Event code: 309-CPA

Task: Observe Career Planner's product knowledge.

Condition: provided with the appropriate references, materials, and equipment.

Standard: Local SOP.

Concept of task: None.

Prerequisites: None.

CRP: 0.54   **Sustainment Interval (months):**

External Support Required: None.

Events updated: None.

Reference(s): Local SOP

Event code: 310-CPA

Task: Analyze Career Planner's product knowledge.

Condition: provided with the appropriate references, materials, and equipment.

Standard: Local SOP.

Concept of task: None.

Prerequisites: None.

CRP: 0.81   **Sustainment Interval (months):**

External Support Required: None.

Events updated: None.

Reference(s): Local SOP

Event code: 311-CPA

Task: Observe Career Planner's communication skills.

Condition: Provided with the appropriate references, materials, and equipment.

Standard: Local SOP.

Concept of task: None.

Prerequisites: None.

CRP: 0.27   **Sustainment Interval (months):**

External Support Required: None.

Events updated: None.

Reference(s): Local SOP

Event code: 312-CPA

Task: Observe Career Planner's administrative skills.

Condition: Provided with the appropriate references, materials, and equipment.

Standard: Per the appropriate references.

Concept of task: None.

Prerequisites: None.

CRP: 0.54 **Sustainment Interval (months):**

External Support Required: None.

Events updated: None.

Reference(s): MCO P1040.31, Enlisted Career Planning and Retention Manual
MCO P1040R.35, Reserve Career Planning and Retention Manual
Local SOP

Event code: 313-CPA

Task: Observe Career Planner's Marine management skills.

Condition: Provided with the appropriate references, materials, and equipment.

Standard: Local SOP.

Concept of task: None.

Prerequisites: None.

CRP: 0.27 **Sustainment Interval (months):**

External Support Required: None.

Events updated: None.

Reference(s): Local SOP

Event code: 314-CPA

Task: Develop supportive Career Planning product knowledge.

Condition: Provided with the appropriate references, materials, and equipment.

Standard: Local SOP.

Concept of task: None.

Prerequisites: None.

CRP: 0.27 **Sustainment Interval (months):**

External Support Required: None.

Events updated: None.

Reference(s): Local SOP

Event code: 315-CPA

Task: Develop supportive Career Planning communication skills.

Condition: Provided with the appropriate references, materials, and equipment.

Standard: Local SOP.

Concept of task: None.

Prerequisites: None.

CRP: 0.27 **Sustainment Interval (months)**:

External Support Required: None.

Events updated: None.

Reference(s): Local SOP

Event code: 316-CPA

Task: Develop supportive Career Planning time management skills.

Condition: Provided with the appropriate references, materials, and equipment.

Standard: Local SOP.

Concept of task: None.

Prerequisites: Nonc.

CRP: 0.81 **Sustainment Interval (months)**:

External Support Required: None.

Events updated: None.

Reference(s): Local SOP

Event code: 317-CPA

Task: Analyze Career Planners time management skills.

Condition: provided with the appropriate references, materials, and equipment.

Standard: Local SOP.

Concept of task: None.

Prerequisites: None.

CRP: 0.81 **Sustainment Interval (months)**:

External Support Required: None.

Events updated: None.

Reference(s): Local SOP

Event code: 318-CPA

Task: Analyze Career Planner's communication skills.

Condition: Provided with the appropriate references, materials, and equipment.

Standard: Local SOP.

Concept of task: None.

Prerequisites: None.

CRP: 0.54 **Sustainment Interval (months):**

External Support Required: None.

Events updated: None.

Reference(s): Local SOP

Event code: 319-CPA

Task: Analyze Career Planner's administrative skills.

Condition: Provided with the appropriate references, materials, and equipment.

Standard: Per the appropriate references.

Concept of task: None.

Prerequisites: None.

CRP: 0.81 **Sustainment Interval (months):**

External Support Required: None.

Events updated: None.

Reference(s): Local SOP
MCO P1040.31, Enlisted Career Planning and Retention Manual
MCO P1040R.35, Reserve Career Planning and Retention Manual
SECNAVINST 5216.5, Correspondence Manual
MCO P1070.12, Marine Corps Individual Records
Administration Manual (IRAM)
MCO P1001R.1, Marine Corps Reserve Administration
Management Manual (MCRMMM)

Event code: 320-CPA

Task: Conduct service level Career Planner information briefs.

Condition: Provided with the appropriate references, materials, and equipment.

Standard: Local SOP.

Concept of task: None.

Prerequisites: None.

CRP: 0.27 **Sustainment Interval (months):**

External Support Required: None.

Events updated: None.

Reference(s): Local SOP

Event code: 321-CPA

Task: Prepare a service level Career Planning related product in the current Marine Corps presentation application.

Condition: Provided with the appropriate references, materials, and equipment.

Standard: Local SOP.

Concept of task: None.

Prerequisites: None.

CRP: 0.54 **Sustainment Interval (months):**

External Support Required: None.

Events updated: None.

Reference(s): Local SOP

Event code: 322-CPA

Task: Prepare a service level Career Planning related product in the current Marine Corps database application.

Condition: Provided with the appropriate references, materials, and equipment.

Standard: Local SOP.

Concept of task: None.

Prerequisites: None.

CRP: 0.27 **Sustainment Interval (months):**

External Support Required: None.

Events updated: None.

Reference(s): Local SOP

Event code: 323-CPA

Task: Prepare a service level Career Planning related product in the current Marine Corps spreadsheet application.

Condition: Provided with the appropriate references, materials, and equipment.

Standard: Local SOP.

Concept of task: None.

Prerequisites: None.

CRP: 0.27 **Sustainment Interval (months):**

External Support Required: None.

Events updated: None.

Reference(s): Local SOP

Event code: 324-CPA

Task: Prepare a service level Career Planning related product in the current Marine Corps word processing application.

Condition: provided with the appropriate references, materials, and equipment.

Standard: Local SOP.

Concept of task: None.

Prerequisites: None.

CRP: 0.27 **Sustainment Interval (months):**

External Support Required: None.

Events updated: None.

Reference(s): Local SOP

Event code: 325-CPP

Task: Produce Career Planning report.

Condition: Provided with the appropriate references, materials, and equipment.

Standard: Local SOP.

Concept of task: None.

Prerequisites: None.

CRP: 0.81 **Sustainment Interval (months):** 1

External Support Required: None.

Events updated: None.

Reference(s): Local SOP

Event code: 326-CPP

Task: Conduct quality control of RELMs.

Condition: Provided with the appropriate references, materials, and equipment.

Standard: Per the appropriate references.

Concept of task: None.

Prerequisites: None.

CRP: 0.81 **Sustainment Interval (months):** 1

External Support Required: None.

Events updated: None.

Reference(s): MCO P1040.31, Enlisted Career Planning and Retention Manual
MCO P1040R.35, Reserve Career Planning and Retention Manual
Local SOP

Event code: 327-CPR

Task: Conduct quality control of the Selected Reserve Referral Program.

Condition: Provided with the appropriate references, materials, and equipment.

Standard: Per the appropriate references.

Concept of task: None.

Prerequisites: None.

CRP: 0.27 **Sustainment Interval (months):** 12

External Support Required: None.

Events updated: None.

Reference(s): MCO P1040R.35, Reserve Career Planning and Retention Manual
MCO 1130.56, Total Force Recruiting

Event code: 328-CPP

Task: Author a Naval message.

Condition: Provided with the appropriate references, materials, and equipment.

Standard: Per appropriate references.

Concept of task: None.

Prerequisites: None.

CRP: 0.27 **Sustainment Interval (months):** 3

External Support Required: None.

Events updated: None.

Reference(s): SECNAVINST 5216.5, Correspondence Manual
MCO P1040.31, Enlisted Career Planning and Retention Manual
MCO P1040R.35, Reserve Career Planning and Retention Manual

Event code: 329-CPP

Task: Conduct liaison between subordinate commands and higher headquarters.

Condition: Provided with the appropriate references, materials, and equipment.

Standard: Local SOP.

Concept of task: None.

Prerequisites: None.

CRP: 0.27 **Sustainment Interval (months)**: .5

External Support Required: None.

Events updated: None.

Reference(s): Local SOP

Event code: 330-CPP

Task: Quality control the request for a waiver of reenlistment prerequisites.

Condition: Provided with the appropriate references, materials, and equipment.

Standard: Per the appropriate references.

Concept of task: None.

Prerequisites: None.

CRP: 0.54 **Sustainment Interval (months)**: 3

External Support Required: None.

Events updated: None.

Reference(s): MCO P1040.31, Enlisted Career Planning and Retention Manual
Local SOP

Event code: 331-CPR

Task: Quality control the Reserve Sponsorship Program.

Condition: Provided with the appropriate references, materials, and equipment.

Standard: Per the appropriate references.

Concept of task: None.

Prerequisites: None.

CRP: 0.27 **Sustainment Interval (months)**: 12

External Support Required: None.

Events updated: None.

Reference(s): MCO P1040R.35, Reserve Career Planning and Retention Manual
MCO 1130.56, Total Force Recruiting

Event code: 332-CPP

Task: Analyze Career Planning data.

Condition: Provided with the appropriate references, materials, and equipment.

Standard: Per the appropriate references.

Concept of task: None.

Prerequisites: None.

CRP: 0.81   **Sustainment Interval (months):** 1

External Support Required: None.

Events updated: None.

Reference(s): MCO P1040.31, Enlisted Career Planning and Retention Manual
MCO P1040R.35, Reserve Career Planning and Retention Manual
Local SOP

Event code: 333-CPP

Task: Advise the commander on matters pertaining to enlisted retention.

Condition: Provided with the appropriate references, materials, and equipment.

Standard: Per the appropriate references.

Concept of task: None.

Prerequisites: None.

CRP: 0.81   **Sustainment Interval (months):**

External Support Required: None.

Events updated: None.

Reference(s): MCO P1040.31, Enlisted Career Planning and Retention Manual
MCO P1040R.35, Reserve Career Planning and Retention Manual
Local SOP

Event code: 334-CPP

Task: Implement FTAP within your command.

Condition: Provided with the appropriate references, materials, and equipment.

Standard: Local SOP.

Concept of task: None.

Prerequisites: None.

CRP: 0.81   **Sustainment Interval (months):** 12

External Support Required: None.

Events updated: None.

Reference(s): Local SOP

Event code: 335-CPP

Task: Coordinate requirement of visiting agencies supporting Career Planning.

Condition: Provided with the appropriate references, materials, and equipment.

Standard: Local SOP.

Concept of task: None.

Prerequisites: None.

CRP: 0.27 **Sustainment Interval (months):** 6

External Support Required: None.

Events updated: None.

Reference(s): Local SOP

Event code: 336-CPP

Task: Implement the Retention Campaign Plan.

Condition: Provided with the appropriate references, materials, and equipment.

Standard: Local SOP.

Concept of task: None.

Prerequisites: None.

CRP: 0.81 **Sustainment Interval (months):** 12

External Support Required: None.

Events updated: None.

Reference(s): Local SOP

Event code: 337-CPR

Task: Quality control the request for an on-contract waiver of reenlistment prerequisites.

Condition: provided with the appropriate references, materials, and equipment.

Standard: MCO P1040R.35, Reserve Career Planning and Retention Manual.

Concept of task: None.

Prerequisites: None.

CRP: 0.54 **Sustainment Interval (months):** 6

External Support Required: None.

Events updated: None.

Reference(s):   MCO P1040R.35, Reserve Career Planning and Retention Manual

Event code: 338-CPP

Task: Conduct a 3, 6, and 9 month evaluation of subordinate Career Planners.

Condition: Provided with the appropriate references, materials, and equipment.

Standard: Local SOP.

Concept of task: None.

Prerequisites: None.

CRP: 0.81   **Sustainment Interval (months):**   3

External Support Required: None.

Events updated: None.

Reference(s):   Local SOP

Event code: 339-CPA

Task: Explain the elements to consider when conducting a 3, 6, and 9 month evaluation of subordinate Career Planners.

Condition: Provided with the appropriate references, materials, and equipment.

Standard: Local SOP.

Concept of task: None.

Prerequisites: None.

CRP: 0.81   **Sustainment Interval (months):**   3

External Support Required: None.

Events updated: None.

Reference(s):   Local SOP

Event code: 340-CPP

Task: Provide guidance on service level retention matters.

Condition: Provided with the appropriate references, materials, and equipment.

Standard: Local SOP.

Concept of task: None.

Prerequisites: None.

CRP: 0.81 **Sustainment Interval (months):** 1

External Support Required: None.

Events updated: None.

Reference(s): Local SOP

Event code: 341-CPP

Task: Manage lateral move school seats.

Condition: Provided with the appropriate references, materials, and equipment.

Standard: MCO 1220.5, Enlisted Lateral Movement.

Concept of task: None.

Prerequisites: None.

CRP: 0.54 **Sustainment Interval (months):** 1

External Support Required: None.

Events updated: None.

Reference(s): MCO 1220.5, Enlisted Lateral Movement

Event code: 342-CPP

Task: Manage the Incentive School Seat Program.

Condition: Provided with the appropriate references, materials, and equipment.

Standard: Per the appropriate references.

Concept of task: None.

Prerequisites: None.

CRP: 0.27 **Sustainment Interval (months):** 3

External Support Required: None.

Events updated: None.

Reference(s): Local SOP

Event code: 343-CPP

Task: Reclassify Marines with revoked MOS.

Condition: Provided with the appropriate references, materials, and equipment.

Standard: Per the appropriate references.

Concept of task: None.

Prerequisites: None.

CRP: 0.27 **Sustainment Interval (months):** 3

External Support Required: None.

Events updated: None.

Reference(s): MCO 1220.5, Enlisted Lateral Movement

Event code: 344-CPP

Task: Authorize telephonic extensions.

Condition: provided with the appropriate references, materials, and equipment.

Standard: Per the appropriate references.

Concept of task: None.

Prerequisites: None.

CRP: 0.54 **Sustainment Interval (months):** .5

External Support Required: None.

Events updated: None.

Reference(s): MCO P1040.31, Enlisted Career Planning and Retention Manual
MCO P1040R.35, Reserve Career Planning and Retention Manual

Event code: 345-CPP

Task: Provide assistance to users interacting with the TFRS database In Career Planning matters.

Condition: Provided with the appropriate references, materials, and equipment.

Standard: MCO P1040.31, Enlisted Career Planning and Retention Manual.

Concept of task: None.

Prerequisites: None.

CRP: 0.81 **Sustainment Interval (months):** 1

External Support Required: None.

Events updated: None.

Reference(s): MCO P1040.31, Enlisted Career Planning and Retention Manual

Event code: 346-CPR

Task: Advise the RAM-2 monitor on Active Reserve (AR) assignments in Career Planner billets.

Condition: Provided with the appropriate references, materials, and equipment.

Standard: Per the appropriate references.

Concept of task: None.

Prerequisites: None.

CRP: 0.27   **Sustainment Interval (months):** 3

External Support Required: None.

Events updated: None.

Reference(s):   MCO P1040R.35, Reserve Career Planning and Retention Manual
MCO 1001.52, Marine Corps Reserve Active Reserve(AR) Program in Support of the Reserve Component

Event code: 347-CPR

Task: Assign SMCR Marines to Career Planner billets.

Condition: Provided with the appropriate references, materials, and equipment.

Standard: MCO P1040R.35, Reserve Career Planning and Retention Manual

Concept of task: None.

Prerequisites: None.

CRP: 0.54   **Sustainment Interval (months):** 12

External Support Required: None.

Events updated: None.

Reference(s):   MCO P1040R.35, Reserve Career Planning and Retention Manual

CHAPTER 1

APPENDIX H

SECTION TRAINING (400 LEVEL)

Purpose: The purpose of the 400 level is to identify those tasks which are completed by the section. These tasks are directly tied to the core competencies listed for this MOS.

Administrative Notes: None.

Prerequisites: None.

CHAPTER 1

Event code: 400-CPP

Task: Process a RELM request.

Condition: provided with the appropriate references, materials, and equipment.

Standard: Per the appropriate references.

Concept of task: None.

Prerequisites: None.

CRP: 0.25   **Sustainment Interval (months):** 3

External Support Required: None.

Events updated: None.

Reference(s): MCO P1040.31, Enlisted Career Planning and Retention Manual
MCO P1040R.35, Reserve Career Planning and Retention
Manual Local SOP

Event code: 401-CPP

Task: Process Prior Service Enlistment Program (PSEP) packages.

Condition: Provided with the appropriate references, materials, and equipment.

Standard: Per the appropriate references.

Concept of task: None.

Prerequisites: None.

CRP: 0.25   **Sustainment Interval (months):** 3

External Support Required: None.

Events updated: None.

Reference(s): MCO P1040.31, Enlisted Career Planning and Retention Manual
MCO P1O4OR.35, Reserve Career Planning and Retention Manual
MCO 1130.58, Reenlistment of Prior Service Marines and
Augmentation of Marine Corps Reservist into the Marine
Corps
Local SOP

Event code: 402-CPP

Task: Maintain the boat space report.

Condition: Provided with the appropriate references, materials, and equipment.

Standard: Per the appropriate references.

Concept of task: None.

Prerequisites: None.

CRP: 0.25   **Sustainment Interval (months):** 3

External Support Required: None.

Events updated: None.

Reference(s): MCO P1040.31, Enlisted Career Planning and Retention Manual
MCO P1040R.35, Reserve Career Planning and Retention Manual
Local SOP

Event code: 404-CPP

Task: Publish guidance pertaining to retention matters.

Condition: Provided with the appropriate references, materials, and equipment.

Standard: Per the appropriate references.

Concept of task: None.

Prerequisites: None.

CRP: 0.25 **Sustainment Interval (months)**: 3

External Support Required: None.

Events updated: None.

Reference(s): MCO P1040.31, Enlisted Career Planning and Retention Manual
MCO P1040R.35, Reserve Career Planning and Retention Manual
Local SOP

Course Title Title	Location	Designation
None.		

Level	Academic Title
200	7 Habits of Highly Effective People, Stephen R. Covey.
200	Technical writing, Local College.
200	Public Speaking, Local College.
200	Punctuation, MCI.
200	Spelling, MCI.
200	TAP/TAMP, Local Base/Station.
200	Instructor Orientation Course, Instructor Management School, Camp Pendleton/Camp Lejeune.
200	Basic Correspondence, MCI.
200	English Composition 101, Local University.
200	Computer applications training, Local Base/Station.

CHAPTER 1

APPENDIX K

CAREER PROFESSIONAL READING

Level	Reading
200	7 Habits of Highly Effective People, Stephen R. Covey.
200	Over the Top, Zig zigglar.
200	Marine Gazette.
200	Marine Corps Times.

Event	Events Updated
100-CPC	None.
101-CPC	None.
102-CPC	None.
103-CPC	None.
104-CPC	None.
105-CPC	None.
106-CPC	None.
107-CPC	None.
108-CPC	None.
110-CPC	None.
111-CPR	None.
112-CPC	None.
113-CPC	None.
114-CPC	None.
115-CPC	None.
116-CPC	None.
117-CPC	None.
118-CPC	None.
119-CPC	None.
120-CPC	None.
121-CPC	None.
122-CPC	None.
123-CPC	None.
124-CPC	None.
125-CPC	None.
126-CPC	None.
127-CPC	None.
128-CPC	None.
129-CPC	None.

Event	Events Updated
130-CPC	None.
131-CPC	None.
132-CPC	None.
133CPC	None.
134-CPC	None.
135-CPC	None.
136CPC	None.
137-CPC	None.
138-CPC	None.
139-CPC	None.
140-CPC	None.
141-CPC	None.
142-CPR	None.
143-CPC	None.
144-CPC	None.
145-CPC	None.
146-CPR	None.
147-CPC	None.
148-CPC	None.
149-CPC	None.
150-CPC	None.
151-CPC	None.
153-CPC	None.
154-CPC	None.
155-CPC	None.
156-CPC	None.
157-CPC	None.
158-CPC	None.
159-CPC	None.
160-CPC	None.
161-CPC	None.
162-CPC	None.

Event	Events Updated
163-CPC	None.
164-CPC	None.
165-CPC	None.
166-CPC	None.
167-CPC	None.
168-CPC	None.
169-CPC	None.
170-CPC	None.
171-CPC	None.
172-CPC	None.
173-CPC	None.
174-CPC	None.
175-CPC	None.
176-CPC	None.
177-CPC	None.
178-CPC	None.
179-CPC	None.
180-CPC	None.
181-CPC	None.
182-CPC	None.
183-CPC	None.
184-CPC	None.
185-CPC	None.
186-CPC	None.
187-CPC	None.
188-CPC	None.
189-CPC	None.
190-CPC	None.
191-CPC	None.
192-CPC	None.
193-CPC	None.
194-CPC	None.

Event	Events Updated
200-CPC	None.
201-CPC	None.
202-CPC	None.
203-CPC	None.
204-CPR	None.
205-CPC	None.
206-CPC	None.
207-CPC	None.
208-CPC	None.
209-CPC	None.
210-CPC	None.
211-CPC	None.
212-CPC	None.
213-CPC	None.
214-CPC	None.
215-CPC	None.
216-CPC	None.
217-CPC	None.
218-CPC	None.
219-CPC	None.
220-CPR	None.
221-CPC	None.
222-CPC	None.
223-CPC	None.
224-CPC	None.
225-CPC	None.
226-CPC	None.
227-CPC	None.
228-CPC	None.
229-CPC	None.
230-CPC	None.
231-CPR	None.

L-4

Event	Events Updated
232-CPR	None.
233-CPR	None.
234-CPR	None.
235-CPC	None.
236-CPC	None.
237-CPC	None.
238-CPC	None.
239-CPC	None.
240-CPC	None.
241-CPC	None.
242-CPC	None.
243-CPC	None.
244-CPC	None.
245-CPC	None.
246-CPC	None.
247-CPC	None.
248-CPC	None.
249-CPR	None.
250-CPC	None.
251-CPC	None.
252-CPC	None.
253-CPC	None.
300-CPA	None.
301-CPA	None.
302-CPA	None.
303-CPA	None.
304-CPA	None.
305-CPA	None.
306-CPA	None.
307-CPA	None.
308-CPA	None.
309-CPA	None.

Event	Events Updated
310-CPA	None.
311-CPA	None.
312-CPA	None.
313-CPA	None.
314-CPA	None.
315-CPA	None.
316-CPA	None.
317-CPA	None.
318-CPA	None.
319-CPA	None.
320-CPA	None.
321-CPA	None.
322-CPA	None.
323-CPA	None.
324-CPA	None.
325-CPP	None.
326-CPP	None.
327-CPR	None.
328-CPP	None.
329-CPP	None.
330-CPP	None.
331-CPR	None.
332-CPP	None.
333-CPP	None.
334-CPP	None.
335-CPP	None.
336-CPP	None.
337-CPR	None.
338-CPP	None.
339-CPA	None.
340-CPP	None.
341-CPP	None.

Event	Events Updated
342-CPP	None.
343-CPP	None.
344-CPP	None.
345-CPP	None.
346-CPR	None.
347-CPR	None.
400-CPP	None.
401-CPP	None.
402-CPP	None.
404-CPP	None.

L-7

Billet	Formal School
None.	

AMMUNITION REQUIREMENTS

DODIC	Quantity	Event code
None.		

Department of Defense Financial Management Regulation (DODFMR)

MCO 1001.39, Counseling of Enlisted Personnel being Separated from Active Duty in the Marine Corps Concerning Participation in the Marine Corps Reserve

MCO 1040.42, Marine Corps Limited Duty Officer/Warrant Officer(LDO/WO) Program

MCO 1040.43, Enlisted to Officer Commissioning Program (ECP/MCP)

MCO 1040R.10, Selected Marine Corps Reserve Direct Commissioning(SMCRDC) Program

MCO 1130.52, Military Personnel Procurement Armed Forced Vocational Testing Program

MCO 1130.55, Prior Service Enlistment Incentive Program

MCO 1130.57, Enlisted Bonus Program (EBP)MCO 1130.58, Reenlistment of Prior

Service Marines and Augmentation of Marine Corps Reservist into the Marine Corps

MCO 1130.63, Enlisted/Reenlistment of Reserve SNCO and Officers/Former Officers in the Regular USMC

MCO 1220.5, Enlisted Lateral Movement

MCO 1500R.36, Training/Category P Program

CHAPTER 1

MCO 1530.11, Naval Academy/Naval Preparatory School

MCO 1550.22, Marine Corps Apprenticeship Program

MCO 1550.23, Military Academic Skills Program (MASP)

MCO 1560.15, Marine Corps Enlisted Commissioning Education Program (MECEP)

MCO 1560.21, Degree Completion Program for Staff Noncommissioned Officers

MCO 1560.24, Broodened Opportunity for Officer Selection and Training Program (BOOST)

MCO 1560.26, Marine Corps Tuition Assistance Program

MCO 1560.28, Veterans Educational Assistance Program (VEAP)

MCO 1560R.30, Selected Reserve Montgomery GI Bill (MGIB-R)

MCO 1610.11, Performance Evaluation Appeals

MCO 1741.9, Retired Serviceman's Family Protection Plan

MCO 5000.12, Marine Corps Policy and Procedures for Pregnant Marines

MCO 5215.1, Marine Corps Directive System

MCO 6100.10, weight Control and Military Appearance

MCO 6100.3, Physical Fitness

CHAPTER 1

MCO 7220.12,   Special Duty Assignment Pay Program

MCO 7220.24,   Selective Reenlistment Bonus Program (SRBP)

MCO 7220.31, Joint Uniform Military Pay System Field Procedures Manual

MCO P1000.6, Assignment, Classification, and Travel Systems Manual(ACTS MAN)

MCO P1001R.1, Marine Corps Reserve Administration Management Manual(MCRMMM)

MCO P1040.31, Enlisted Career Planning and Retention Manual

MCO P1040R.35, Reserve Career Planning and Retention Manual

MCO P1050.3, Leave and Liberty Manual

MCO P1070.12, Marine Corps Individual Records Administration Manual(IRAM)

MCO P1080.20, Marine Corps Total Force Codes Manual (MCTFSCODESMAN)

MCO P1080.35, Personnel Reporting Instructions Manual (PRIM)

MCO P1200.7, Military Occupational Specialities Manual (MOS Manual)

MCO P1400.32, Enlisted Promotion Manual

MCO P1400.32, Marine Corps Promotion Manual, Volume 2, Enlisted Promotions (MARCORPROMAN, VOL 2, ENLPROM)

MCO P1610.7, Performance Evaluation System (PES)

MCO P1741.11, Survivor Benefit Plan

MCO P1080.40, MCTFSPRIM

MCO P1900.16, Marine Corps Separation and Retirement Manual (SEPMAN)

MCO P7220.31, Joint Uniform Military Pay System Field Procedures Manual

OPNAVINST 1780.2, Montgomery GI Bill (NOTAL)

SECNAVINST 5210.11, Standard Subject Identification Codes (SSIC) Manual

SECNAVINST 5216.5, Correspondence Manual